c. 2015

Praise for *Thi:*

Diane's story left m ....ers nope to every parent of a child with special needs. Although born with spina bifida, Diane broke through her limitations to live a full life with a career, family and numerous interests and involvements. Her experiences allowed me to look at life through the lens of an adolescent, like my daughter who has spina bifida, and to see my actions from her perspective. I also found myself connecting with her parents' story, as they struggled to care for her at a time when resources and information were limited. I will read this book again and again and hope my daughter does as well. We all can learn from Diane's journey to dance into the light of courage and resilience of the human spirit.

Megan Sorensen
Chair, Board of Directors
Spina Bifida Association of America

Personal stories can touch us in deeply meaningful ways. In many ways, Diane's story is every woman's story. While many aspects of it are unique to her, we will recognize the common themes that will intersect with our own experiences and understandings.

Kathy Reardon, RN, MS, Holistic Nurse
and Spiritual Director

"This book tells an important part of the story of what it means to grow up with a disability and to address issues of dependence and frailty, wellness and healing."

Terry Schupbach-Gordon, artist, storyteller, disability
advocate, and co-director of Catbird (on the Yadkin) Press

This beautifully written book, *This Need to Dance*, will give you courage for the journey, whether you are facing a debilitating physical or mental condition, or the normal challenges of daily life. In this account of her struggles over the years with spina bifida and, later, cancer, Diane Glass shows us what resilience is all about: searching deep inside yourself for strengths you did not know you had; accepting with gratitude the help of fellow travelers; being open to unexpected gifts, from unexpected sources; and keeping a gentle sense of humor along the way.

Nancy L. Jones, Ph.D., Director, Writing Resource Center, University of Iowa College of Law

"This story of discoveries speaks to Diane Glass's gifts — clarity, deep strength and resilience. We watch those qualities emerge through decades of dealing with the frailty that is spina bifida and the fear that is cancer. From creating the mystic beauty of Ravel on her Steinway to considering a life without dancing, from the confines of structured religion to finally finding a comfortable Jesus who'd always been waiting, she invites us along on this most unusual journey. Profoundly honest, this private woman shares the river and all its tributaries that carried her physically and spiritually to acceptance, purpose and joy."

Mary Kay Shanley, Iowa Author of the Year, Co-Facilitator of Women's Writing Retreats

It is rare to learn the "secrets" of illness and disease in such a public venue. This book breaks down barriers and brings light to aspects of personhood and sexuality that have previously been secluded in darkness. What a gift.

Dr. Norma J. Hirsch. MD
Osteopathic Medicine, Des Moines University

This Need to Dance

A Life of Rhythm and Resilience

This Need to Dance

A Life of Rhythm and Resilience

by

Diane Glass

Zion Publishing

Des Moines, Iowa

Edited by Mary Ylvisaker Nilsen of Zion Publishing
Cover design by Mary Ylvisaker Nilsen
Cover Photography by Brent Isenberger of Brent Isenberger Photography, Des Moines IA
Chapter graphic by downimage and used with permission.

ISBN-13: 978-1512332612
ISBN-10: 1512332615

For discounted bulk orders, contact the author:
dianeglass96@gmail.com

www.dianeeglass.com

Published by Zion Publishing
Des Moines IA

To my mother and father

Dear Sarah,
I hope you enjoy
the book. May
your spirit always
dance!
Liane

Of Being

I know this happiness
is provisional:
> the looming presences—
> great suffering, great fear—

> withdraw only
> into peripheral vision.

But ineluctable this shimmering
of wind in the blue heavens

this flood of stillness widening the lake of
sky:

this need to dance,
this need to kneel:
> this mystery:

by Denise Levertov

"When the music changes, so does the
dance."

African Proverb

Table of Contents

Dance for Us

I heard a friend call out, "Dance for us!" We were in the party room of a small Thai restaurant in the warehouse district of Des Moines. We had gathered to surprise my husband Jeff on his 70th birthday.

"Yes, dance," someone else called lightheartedly. "Show us what you've learned in your ballroom dance lessons."

Tables laden with Pad Thai, sushi rolls, cashew chicken and yellow curry limited the space available for dancing. Undaunted I flung out my arms with exaggerated drama and twirled my skirt in invitation to Jeff sitting nearby. Hesitating only a moment, he stepped carefully through the dining tables. His arm circled my waist and together we assumed the dance position we had learned. Without a whisper of communication, we started to do the double-time swing.

The tune to "I can't give you anything but

love" ran through my mind as we synchronized our steps and danced without benefit of music. One-two-three, one-two-three. One-two…. We did under arms turns, the cuddle-up, and the hand exchange and were about to tackle the whip when our guests broke into applause — Jeff's colleagues, our dinner club members, my writing group companions, family members including my sister Susie who had come from Texas, Jeff's sister Ann, and even Jeff's son Tim, my stepson, who had been struggling with mental illness since he was a teenager. But that night, he was present, smiling and swaying to our imaginary music. Aaron, our other son, and his wife Saraswati with their two-year-old son Soma arrived soon after.

I occasionally leaned on Jeff's arm to keep from stumbling. My rubber-soled comfort shoes — not ideal for dancing — kept me from gliding gracefully. But I refused to let that bother me, and I savored the moment. Jeff was nearing completion of a forty-year career as a counselor at the Des Moines Pastoral Counseling Center he had helped to grow and as a member of the faculty of Des Moines University. After leaving my newspaper-marketing career, I had chosen a new vocation in spiritual direction and it had blossomed. We were close to celebrating our twenty-year wedding anniversary. And, after two near-fatal encounters with illness, I was not only alive but also dancing with gratitude.

Born with spina bifida at a time when few babies survived this birth defect, I was cautiously carried out of the hospital by my parents and taken home to die. The doctor who attended my delivery advised them that the best course of action was to make me as comfortable as possible in the days, weeks or perhaps months ahead. However, apparently, even as an infant, I had a mind of my own. I chose to live.

While this memoir will address how I learned to live with spina bifida and then fought breast cancer, it is not a story about physical illness. Rather, it is an account of what and how I learned from the life struggles I faced. How secrecy can protect us initially as we hide things we would rather others not know, but how, in the long-term, such secrecy undermines our confidence and sense of self-worth. How well-meaning parents and doctors guide and treat us to the best of their knowledge and how unexpected helping hands intervene at critical moments to address seemingly unsolvable problems. How imagination and curiosity support us as we maneuver circumstances that can be overwhelming. How we can do all the right things and still not be successful. How it is often unclear what the right thing is, leaving us to muddle through. How ultimately, we work with whatever our life presents in pursuit of the happiness we all seek.

Looking back I see that, all together, these dispositions of attitude and behavior, of mind and heart, created a certain inner rhythm — a dance that has allowed me to have a full, abundant life.

Jeff was my second marriage and I his. A mutual enjoyment of dancing drew us together. We were an unlikely-looking dance couple, he short and pleasantly round with a teddy bear look and me taller and dramatic with swaying skirts and dangling jewelry. Dancing required him to lead, challenging his humble and sometimes self-effacing manner. I always needed to tame my tendency to take charge. No matter how awkward we might have looked, we loved to experience a shared rhythm and a growing appreciation for what the other brought to our mutual life dance.

Dance was, for me, more than a synchronized physical movement to music. Dance was my life. Or perhaps better to say, my life was like dance. As in dance, I surrendered the lead when something beyond my control happened. When no one took the lead, I stepped up and forward and took charge to the best of my ability. When opportunities came to display my talents, I took them. When illness prevented my doing so, I reluctantly worked through the grief of letting go. Yes, my life had rhythm but it was a rhythm orchestrated by life itself—by the condition of my body, by the people around me, by situations I created and those that just happened, by my own growing awareness of what was valuable and important.

This willingness and ability to respond to life's

ever-changing rhythms has served me well. It has helped me survive embarrassing moments with my leaky bladder, recover from ill-advised romantic relationships, relish career successes and accept failures, and navigate family struggles and bodily challenges some might say are better not discussed.

In fact, as I wrote, I could almost hear my dad's voice saying, "Diane, some things are best not talked about outside the family." Yet, I share these happenings without embarrassment or judgment. In doing so, I seek to release whatever hold these stories still have, to forgive myself and everyone involved, and to live with greater peace.

Every chapter begins with a recent life experience. These are for the most part chronological — from 1999 to the present time. The more current stories wrap their arms around each chapter's body — events from my earlier life that have both sustained and haunted me all these years.

For much of my life, I thought of myself as different, set apart by the surgical scars on my back and impaired bladder, which I kept as a dark secret. But I have come to realize that we all in one way or another live with "the looming presences — great suffering, great fear" of Denise Levertov's poem in the epigraph. What sustains me in the midst of life's vagaries is the "ineluctable shimmering" she posits — and that I experience. That shimmering, that mystery that takes my imagination and my heart beyond immediate setback and invites me into life with anticipation and hope. This is my need to dance, to claim with open arms the beauty and joy of this one lifetime.

Whether you think of yourself as a dancer or not, I invite you to consider how the music of life—yours as well as mine—calls us to move forward and then back, to find our rhythm for facing myriad circumstances, to invent new steps, to draw upon our inner strength, and ultimately to hear this melody, this mystery that invites us to a dance of gratitude.

2 You Can't Tell

Iknew sharing personal information is what people do at support groups—they reveal what is often secret in other parts of their lives. But, yikes… I wasn't ready for this.

"Let's all introduce ourselves and get better acquainted. I'm Tina and I had a lumpectomy and radiation earlier this year." The facilitator of the After Breast Cancer group flashed a big grin and swooped her arms in an all-inclusive welcoming gesture. I squirmed in my seat, my back already aching.

She looked at the woman to her right. "Your turn."

"I'm Rhonda and I had a mastectomy, no radiation."

Other women followed this lead, each describing the removal of all or part of one or both breasts. My chest, still tender from recent surgery and covered with soft cotton, concaved even more.

Diagnosed with breast cancer only a month earlier at age 51, I was new to this business of talking about my health, of sharing intimate details, of trusting others with private information. Yes, I had agreed to come to this support group with my friend Stella, two years out from her diagnosis and treatment. But did I want these strangers to know whether I was missing all or part of one breast? Or if I had no breasts? Or fake breasts? Or some lymph nodes or no lymph nodes? Pulling my purse close, I eyed the door. Could I handle this?

Handling things was what I was good at. What I had always done. What I did then as vice president of marketing at the *Des Moines Register* when the local media called with questions. When, for example, the editor and managing editor abruptly resigned because they were having an affair. When our newspaper carrier was kidnaped and the police had tips, reporters had questions and witnesses had ghoulish leads. When our presses came to a halt during the flood of 1993. I was the calm face, the steady voice with carefully choreographed words, the person who handled things.

I knew what the public had a right to know and what was better left out of the news, what to expose and what to protect, what to disclose and what to keep secret. But I didn't know how to handle this. This was about me.

"Hello, I'm Stella and I had a bilateral mastectomy two years ago," my friend said.

My turn. I put on my "handling things" face, but the quiver in my voice gave me away. I punted. "I'm Diane. I had surgery and am waiting for chemotherapy."

That was as much disclosure I could muster for now.

While the breast cancer diagnosis shocked me, the exposure that followed unsettled me even more. Everyone at the newspaper knew, which meant many people in the community knew as well. KCCI-TV sent flowers and before long, other bouquets covered every surface of the living room. My older sister Eileen took over answering telephone calls from people extending sympathy and offering advice or simply asking questions. My secretary set up a hotline to keep everyone informed about treatment plans.

Caught in the glare of what felt like public scrutiny, I resorted to my marketing director skills, delivering brave renditions to my staff and close friends of how I would manage this disease skillfully, how I already had done my research and how I would stay in control of my own treatment by critically reviewing the recommendations offered by specialists. People remarked how brave, how knowledgeable, how poised I was in the midst of this crisis. If I ever have breast cancer, one friend said, this is how I would like to approach it.

This was the person they knew well, someone who planned carefully, executed thoroughly, and succeeded always. Well, almost always. This new health crisis morphed into a campaign, a campaign for my own survival.

Yet breast cancer marked the beginning of a new awareness: I couldn't do this alone. Little room existed for silence or secrecy this time, unlike my experience with spina bifida, which I was born with in 1947. Breast cancer attracts thousands of supporters for annual marches in our community. Retailers sell products from pajamas to coffee mugs with pink ribbons. The American Cancer Society trains hundreds of mentors called navigators to be companions for newly diagnosed women. Breast cancer is a public disease. My friends wanted to help.

In contrast, my experience with spina bifida was shrouded from public view. Few people beyond my family knew my struggles with this birth defect. With my ability to walk unaffected, I passed as "normal" except for those occasional accidents due to incontinence for which I offered no explanation.

My fear facing cancer arose not only from the prospect of debilitating surgery, chemotherapy, and radiation. Treatment would likely exacerbate existing health issues. Chemotherapy thins bones. Some drugs destroy nerve endings and lead to neuropathy. Toxic drugs strain both the kidneys and bladder. Spina bifida had already significantly impaired these organs and functions in my body. As my fear mounted, a rapid heart rate and shallow breaths drove me in a panic to the local drug store for blood pressure checks, where the monitor showed alarming numbers.

This fear also reflected a deeper knowing. To regain my health, I needed to be open and honest with people who cared about me. But to talk about breast cancer now as if it was my first brush with death, as if I didn't have a long and complicated health history, somehow felt disloyal to my body, a body that had done its best to function all these years. I wouldn't be telling the whole story, the real story. I wouldn't be telling the truth.

Sitting there, surrounded by women deep in the throes of their current struggles with breast cancer and feeling my heart rate rev, my thoughts darted to the past, a past characterized by uncertainty and struggle. I searched for the root of this reflex that my spina bifida be kept a secret, that the most important parts of me remain private. What flashed into my mind was the first day of kindergarten.

D efying the prognosis of the doctors that I would surely die soon after birth and surprising my parents by growing into an active, bright-eyed child, I turned five and what had once been thought impossible was inevitable. I had to leave the shelter of my home. I had to go to school. I had to be separated for the first time from someone who could help me empty my non-functioning bladder, damaged when I was born with an open spine. Having just moved to this northeast Iowa town of Arlington months before in the summer of 1952, we knew only our neighbors next door and the customers Dad came into contact with through his business.

At this juncture, my parents faced questions no one had considered before. Because children with spina bifida didn't usually live long enough, no one had considered how these kids would fare in school, relate to other children, learn to read and write, or develop skills that would allow them to be employed. In the 1950s in rural Iowa, few if any resources existed to help these children or their parents.

In this era, many schools did not have school nurses or child development specialists. Special programs for children with mental or physical disabilities either did not exist or, if they did, they segregated children and gave them less than adequate educations. Perhaps fearful I would not even be allowed to go to school, my parents, to the best of my knowledge, remained silent with teachers about my inability to go to the bathroom by myself.

Adding to the logistical difficulty was the fact that my problem—having to be catheterized several times a day to empty my bladder—was of a personal, intimate nature and to some, it was embarrassing or even disgusting. It was best handled in the privacy of our home with little fanfare. How could I have known that my experience, so ordinary to me, was so unusual, so strange for a little girl barely five years old?

My mother prepared me for this entry into the larger world in the only way she knew how—by making new clothes. To purchase the fabric she needed, my family traveled 15 miles to the Kohl's General Store in Strawberry Point. I anticipated these occasional trips with delight—savoring the sight of bolts of fabric, boxes of shoes, stacks of sweaters and pants and jackets, and coats hanging by size—toddlers, children, adults. The store smelled of cotton and wool, rubber and leather, as rural families crowded in to prepare their kids for school. We bought the red rubber boots here that chafed my legs in the winter and the corduroy slacks we wore underneath our dresses for warmth.

My mother and I stroked the fabrics and studied the colors and textures.

"Mommy, I like this," I pointed to a grape-colored fabric decorated with little lambs. I loved the way the lambs danced freely across the material amidst little tufts of grass and flowers. Mother had already picked out the pattern—a sun-dress with a full gathered skirt and a bolero jacket that had the option of lace trimming. Imagining this dress as I watched my mother sew it on her used Singer machine, I could hardly wait for this new experience called "kindergarten."

The week before school started, she took me to the local barbershop to have my hair cut. Even today I recall from school pictures those uneven bangs hovering half an inch above my eyebrows. She also fashioned without a pattern the new diaper I wore, using several layers of soft cotton, cutting the leg opening high enough to avoid binding, and replacing safety pins with snaps.

I could hardly get to sleep the night before, and popped awake the morning of the first day of school. I got up, Dad emptied my bladder and Mother helped me get dressed. Too excited to eat, I just picked at my oatmeal and bacon and gulped my juice.

Mother and I walked hand in hand to the school that first day. Leaving our small white bungalow with its tall pines on either side of a tiny front porch, we crossed the Main Street mostly empty of cars, strolled through the tall cottonwood trees, past Mrs. Shumway's Gothic house with its peeling paint, and then through an open field and into the back door of the school. We could have chosen the route to the front door but this way was quicker and Mother knew I enjoyed looking up through the trees to the sky. Dad later became a member of the local school board and arranged for a sidewalk to be built for our use. That provision appeared justified at the time, but now I marvel that the board authorized the expense since my sisters and I were the only regular users.

When we got to the school, Mother dropped my hand, opened the door, and motioned for me to go in ahead of her. Parents and children, in a chaotic stream, headed for the kindergarten room.

"Welcome, everyone," Miss Lehman, the kindergarten teacher said. "I've been looking forward to this day all summer!"

We sat in little chairs, mothers and children, with mothers balancing pocketbooks awkwardly on their laps.

"Let's start by singing some songs," she said. She asked for suggestions from the children.

After a long pause, I piped up, "Here Comes Santa Claus," ignoring the fact that it was August. Susie and I had tried to remember the words just the other day. Everyone laughed. The little girl next to me whispered to her mother, "She doesn't know it's not Christmas." As her mother hushed her, I blushed, realizing it's not good to stand out too much. After that, I refrained from spontaneously speaking up again.

When Miss Lehman said goodbye to the mothers, my mother's face whitened. Was she afraid to leave me? Should *I* be afraid? I had rarely been separated from one of my parents. How would I go to the bathroom? Why is she leaving? My mother squeezed my hand and said she'd be back at noon to get me.

Miss Lehman removed half the chairs and the kids gathered around her. We sang more songs and she read us a story about a little girl who wanted to fly like the birds. I loved thinking about her.

My mind traveled to our neighbor's yard that burst with the color of daisies, day lilies, coneflowers, and snapdragons and attracted hummingbirds, dragonflies, goldfinch, orioles and all manner of winged creatures. On warm days, I would lie in the grass looking up, hoping the wispy creatures would buzz over me. What fun it would be to fly, to dance in the wind, to glide over the earth, to look down and see everything from a safe distance. The image cocooned me as my teacher read.

My attention was drawn back to the present when Miss Lehman asked us to pick a rug and stretch out for a short nap. It hardly seemed time to sleep. My mind was alive with pictures, songs, and the presence of all these children. I eased myself down onto my mat, lying on my side, and glanced around from my place on the floor, wondering if they knew I was different. As I shifted my position, I was careful to make sure the skirt of my dress covered my diaper. I feared kids would laugh if they saw a diaper.

After a fifteen-minute rest time, a bell rang and Miss Lehman called out, "Children, it's time for you to go to the bathroom."

She pointed to the restrooms—the girls down the hall to the left, the boys to the right. She dismissed us in groups so we wouldn't all rush at once. I stayed in my chair, hesitating. No one had asked me to go to the bathroom before. Had Mother explained to my teacher I was different?

"Diane, you can go now." Did my teacher actually say these words or did I imagine them, so fearful was I of standing out, confused and embarrassed? I stayed frozen in my seat, alone.

"I don't have to go," I said to her with as much confidence as I could muster, not sure whether I did or not. My parents decided that. Regardless of how my bladder felt, I waited until they were ready to "take care of me," our euphemism for catheterization. In the meantime, Miss Lehman moved on to other tasks, preparing a snack of milk and cookies for us.

I glanced at the clock. Eileen had taught me how to tell time, but I forgot when kindergarten was supposed to be over or when my mother would come back. Soon, I hoped.

Then the teacher told us we had some free playtime. We could do anything we wanted. I walked over to the shelf that held all the books and ran my hand along their spines, longing to read every one of them. Then I noticed the blocks and other building toys, the art supplies, the rhythm instruments. I felt a rush of excitement. There was so much to do, so much to learn.

The other children began to pair up with friends. Who could I play with? No one reached out to me. As a newcomer, I had met only Eddie, who lived next door and was younger than me.

He came over to play with Susie and me when Mother filled the rubber swimming pool in the backyard. Judy, whose house we could see from our bedroom window, invited us once to come view the baby rabbits she found in her yard. But neither Eddy nor Judy was in my class. Otherwise, the only children I knew were my sisters. At the moment, home felt safe and predictable in a way school didn't. Yet here I could discover new things.

I chose a book, something I could do alone, and settled into my chair to look at colorful pictures.

When my mother returned to pick me up, she asked, "How did your morning go?"

"It was okay," I said. "We listened to a story, took a nap, and ate some cookies and milk."

"You got along okay?" she asked, her voice dropping to a whisper.

"Yes," I said, sensing what she was wondering. Although she didn't ask me specifically, I knew she was concerned about whether my bladder had leaked. Fortunately, I was relatively dry.

I assumed that mother had not mentioned my needs to the teacher, perhaps out of a desire to maintain my privacy or maybe because she was too timid to talk about this delicate—or in her mind embarrassing—procedure. I was too young to understand her reluctance, but nevertheless picked up the message that this was not something we talked about.

"There's so much to do here, Mommy," I continued, changing the focus. "I want to play like the other kids."

Relieved that everything had gone okay, she took my hand and we walked home, where everything was reliably predictable. But I looked forward to the excitement of tomorrow.

My mother was a resourceful cook, and in this rural community in the 1950s, people ate a big meal at noon they called dinner, not lunch. She made all her dishes from scratch—beef with big fat noodles, barbecued ribs swimming in a sauce made with lots of ketchup, pot roast with little round potatoes, and cherry Jell-O with fruit cocktail.

On that first day of kindergarten, my dad came home for dinner, as he did every day, from his job at the livestock buying station. Smelling of hog dust and manure, he talked about tough negotiations with farmers over the price he would pay for their hogs, about demands from Rath Packing Company for more hogs, and about gossip around town. He dominated the conversation while my mother quietly provided more food as plates became empty.

Then he pushed his chair back and, "Come along, Diane. We need to take care of you." That was the signal. I went to my parents' bedroom, stretched out on their bed and pulled down my diaper. After scrubbing me, inserting

31

the catheter, draining my bladder and pulling it back out, he gave me a tablespoon of sulfa to prevent infection.

As I lay on the bed staring off into nowhere, waiting for my bladder to empty, I felt reassured by this return to normalcy. Tomorrow would be another day at school, another time of both excitement about this new experience and a time of uncertainty about how to handle the bathroom break. I suspect this was when I began thinking of my bladder as somehow not me. Something I could talk to and negotiate with.

"When the teacher asks us to go, I'm going to pretend I'm OK, but you have to be good and not leak," I said to my bladder. "If I don't tell, everyone will think I'm fine." I made a pact with my bladder. "We will just wait until my parents are present to help us. OK?" My bladder agreed, and like a good partner, behaved as well as it could.

The next day when the teacher announced it was time to go to the bathroom, I decided to go into the bathroom, pay attention to what the other girls were doing and follow their example. I just hoped no one would notice the lack of sound from the stall I was in and ask me about it. What would I say?

I feared that this question—what to say?—would come up again and again. And it did. This time at a family gathering at my grandparents' home one Sunday after Mass. In this two-story white frame house known for its lack of adequate heat, women congregated in the kitchen around the stove for warmth, preparing for the early afternoon meal. My grandmother, aunts, mother and most of the children hung out there, engaging in talk about family, especially kids. Men gathered in the living room, smoking cigars, filling the house with stale aromas, and fretted about the struggles facing area farmers, including the low prices garnered by the hogs they sold.

"It's a snake," squealed one of my cousins as he pulled the catheter from the brown paper bag my parents had brought, anticipating the need to catheterize me after dinner. Running through the house, he dangled the rubber tube menacingly in front of other kids' faces. Then he started tossing it from one shrieking child to the next, all the while taunting, "Diane's got a snake. Diane's got a snake."

I tried to hide, shrinking behind one of the oversized chairs in the room filled with men, sobbing in embarrassment and shame.

"Put that away!" one of the adults yelled. My dad quickly grabbed the tube and stuffed it back in the bag.

The horrified rush with which my dad did this suggested how dark this secret truly was. Neither my grandparents nor my aunts and uncles said anything, sensing that my father wanted no further discussion. For the rest of the afternoon, I ate my food quietly, refused to play, and avoided everyone's questioning eyes and said nothing.

A change of topic at the After Breast Cancer support group pulled me back into the present. I tried to listen as people continued to talk, fearing I would, again, be expected to speak.

"I decided to have reconstruction," offered one woman whose surgery was months ago. "I got tired of taking my breasts out of a drawer."

"Did you have nipples constructed as well?" another woman asked.

"No, I stopped short of that. It meant more surgery...."

Like me, the women in this room faced a life-threatening disease, breast cancer. But in my case, cancer represented not just a new health challenge but a total disruption of my anticipated life trajectory. I expected to die of a problem related to spina bifida. Now cancer came along.

"Are you happy with the way your breasts look?" one woman, contemplating reconstruction, asked of another who had completed her surgery the year before.

"They look natural. Both the same. My husband is pleased and I'm happy," she said. "This doctor is an artist."

This candid exchange amazed me. I wondered if I could ever be this comfortable, this relaxed in talking honestly about myself and especially my body. Not only about my breast that had been removed, or the life-sapping chemotherapy process, but also about bladders and urine and wet pants and fear and mortification. I began to sense how limiting, perhaps even damaging, my reluctance to talk about myself, to hide behind secrecy, was becoming.

"Was that helpful?" Stella asked, as the meeting ended and we walked out the door.

"I learned a lot but perhaps more about myself than breast cancer," I responded without elaborating.

"Call, let's have lunch. Let me come over for a visit and talk with you about taking care of your wound and preparing for chemo," Stella said, putting her arm around my shoulders. She had gone through training to mentor women recently diagnosed with breast cancer.

Feeling this gentle support, a kind of support I had never felt before, I wanted to start talking, not only about breast cancer, but also about my big problem, the problem that defined my sense of myself and, particularly, my body—spina bifida. But what to say? And when? And for what purpose?

WHY DO YOU NOT TALK MORE?

The living room of our home on Grand Avenue, a charming Tudor-style house built in the 1930s, embraced group after group of friends in its light, airy space. Armed with casseroles, balloons, flowers and a genuine desire to be helpful, these friends encouraged me to talk about my cancer, both the practical aspects of treatment and the outlook for the future. Their questions and comments helped me open up with a surprising ease.

"How can we help?"

"What did the lab results show?"

"Do you need a ride to chemotherapy?"

"We have a sign-up sheet for your friends to bring food."

"What's it like to face death?"

"Do you feel God's presence in all this?"

"What's next for you in life?"

For someone who didn't like to talk about herself, I was gifted with an unusually warm and supportive circle of women friends who provided the perfect environment for intimate conversation. I told them about the size of the tumor (large), the six months of chemotherapy, and my surgeon's recommendation that I have a second mastectomy because of the likelihood of recurrence. During those conversations, Jeff was rarely far away. He sat discreetly at the table in our garden room adjacent to the living room— close enough to listen to our conversations but far enough away not to interrupt this talk among friends. But the only time I allowed my tears to flow freely was with my friend Mary and with Jeff.

"This is the worst thing that could happen to someone with spina bifida," I sobbed in the garden room of our home, as Mary unpacked soup and scones she had picked up at a local coffee shop.

"My bones are already thinning. Chemo will further weaken them. I'll have the body of an 80-year old before long."

Mary held my hand, saying nothing.

"And my parents are stricken with grief. They saved me as a baby, only to see me succumb to cancer," I added, providing little detail other than that I had been born with spina bifida.

"What can I do right now to help?" Mary asked, after making a telephone call to cancel her afternoon appointment. "Let's spend the day together, if you like."

Jeff began to leave love notes on the kitchen

counter every morning, a practice that continues to this day.

"Be kind to yourself today."

"You bring such joy to my life."

"I love the way your eyes light up when I return home."

"You make our home such a beautiful and happy place."

All this openness and support made me wonder what life would have been like for my parents and me if we had felt this free to talk about *our* lives, about *my* body, and especially about the challenges posed by my leaky bladder. I might have viewed my situation as unusual and different, but not shameful. My parents would not have been so fearful about whether I would be accepted as normal. And if they had had support, they would have been less burdened by the stresses of caring for a child with health problems. I've never known if they felt any guilt or grief, wondering if things could have been different, but surely such support would have relieved them of any lingering doubts or regrets.

All this wondering and questioning fed an active journaling practice and led to joining a writing group of friends focused on capturing the stories of our lives. This marked the beginning of sharing my childhood experiences and their effect on my life. These friends critiqued my writing. They probed the details of my history and asked the all-important question no one had ever posed: How did this make you feel? I didn't know. But it felt as if I needed first to understand my parents' life journey as it intertwined with mine before I could begin to feel and understand my own.

My sisters and I knew little about the details of Mother and Dad's relationship other than that they wed on July 11, 1941, just across the border from Iowa in the state of Missouri. Only my Aunt Anne was present.

"I can't believe I'm married!" Aunt Anne reported my mother said immediately after the ceremony. I wonder if my mother was delightfully taken with this new stage in her life or if she was dumbfounded to find herself in this position. Aunt Anne, guarded on family matters, declined to elaborate on this question.

My parents' wedding photo shows a beautiful young woman with dark hair, expressive eyes and a big smile, dressed in a tailored two-tone jacket with a string of pearls. She stood next to a slim man, also with dark hair, wearing glasses and a neatly tailored suit, and smiling warmly.

Like many people who came to this country at the turn of the century, my mother's parents desired that their children fit into this new world of America and experience success. My grandfather sent three of four children to college with money he earned by repairing shoes, first in Ottumwa, and later in Cedar Rapids. With education, they would find good careers, he reasoned. For most women, that meant teaching. And that is what my mother and Aunt Anne aimed for.

My mother, Helen Dorothy Popchuck, graduated from the University of Iowa on June 7, 1938 with a degree in Home Economics. A photo taken of her soon after graduation shows a vivacious woman with a dazzling smile standing outside a university building in her sheared lamb coat. Another photo of her standing with a handsome young man in a 1940s era suit surfaced from among her possessions after her death. That same young man drew a sketch of the two of them together, looking like glamorous movie stars.

I idly wondered what had happened to him? Was he someone Mother loved or hoped to marry? Or, simply a relationship that ended when she graduated from college and went to Volga to teach?

Her graduation happened during a steadily growing concern about the war that had broken out both in Germany and in the Far East. The March 13, 1938, *Daily Iowan* social column reported that Marjorie Holmquist of Centerville, South Dakota, spent the weekend with Helen Popchuck of Ottumwa at her home. Alongside that column, a news article reported that Adolf Hitler forced the joining of Germany and Austria and defied the world to challenge his aggression.

The *Daily Iowan* pictured him speaking to "wildly cheering crowds."

The June 7, 1938, *Daily Iowan*, in which Mother's name was listed as receiving her bachelor's degree, displayed the headline, "Japanese War Planes Bomb Crowded Canton for the Ninth Day with an Increasing Death Toll."

At a time in their lives when young adults were typically thinking of finding jobs, getting married and starting families, Mother and Dad must have felt the fear and uncertainty gripping the world. This fear was heightened by their not knowing whether and when the United States would enter the conflict.

Mother's first teaching assignment landed her in Volga, a town of a few hundred people located in a scenic river valley. Not particularly close to any urban area, it offered few cultural or social opportunities for a single young woman whose interests ran to reading and classical music.

My dad, John Joseph Cox, a resident of Volga, attended a year of junior college in nearby Elkader, played baseball on his college team and left to run a gas station. His parents, my grandparents, lost their farm in the Depression and now lived in town.

"Your mother always dressed fashionably," my Aunt Mary, Dad's sister, told me one day.

"Her hats and dresses were the talk of the town," she said. "Your dad noticed her walking home from school every day as she passed by the gas station where he worked."

Dad found a way to meet Mother, perhaps by hanging out in front of the station at the time she typically walked by every day and initiating a conversation.

"Sure is a nice day. Say, do you have a car? Do you need any help with it?" I imagine him saying.

If Mother was as shy then as I experienced her later in life, she probably blushed, mumbled a few words and went on her way. My dad no doubt persisted until they started to date. Their relationship progressed from there. My older sister Eileen was born in 1942, which meant that Mother's public school teaching job ended, because pregnant women were not allowed to teach in that era.

The prospect of a family led to their relocation to Waterloo, where opportunities for employment and a living wage were greater. My dad began work at Carnation delivering milk to support his family. Each morning he got up at 4 a.m. and placed glass bottles encased in a cardboard carrier on doorsteps all across town. He brought them to us too, topped with cream and covered with paper caps. In the afternoon and evening, he worked making cottage cheese for the same company, a job that so sickened him he declined to eat cottage cheese or anything resembling it until he died. Eventually, after putting his name on a wait list, he was hired for a better-paying job at Rath Packing Company on the kill line, cutting the cattle and hog carcasses that traveled down the conveyor belts.

On June 15, 1944, he was drafted to serve in WWII, during which time Mother moved back to her parents' home in Ottumwa and taught home economics at Ottumwa High School. After the war, the young couple returned to Waterloo and Dad resumed his job at Rath Packing Company. In 1951, he was offered a promotion at Rath as a livestock buyer and he and Mother moved to Arlington, Iowa.

Most of the people who could fill in the blanks on this story, if they would, are gone. What I know is that Mother and Dad married and began life in the shadow of World War II. I sometimes wonder if they married out of love because their marriage, as I witnessed it, never felt like a good fit. Yet children rarely understand their parents' marriage. One brief interchange sticks in my mind.

Mother is crying.

"You girls know that I love your mother, don't you?" Dad says, more of a statement than a question.

We are silent.

Mother rushes into the bedroom and shuts the door. That ends this out-in-the-open conversation. Who were we to intervene in what felt like an argument, a rare drama enacted before our eyes?

As Dad's involvement in the community grew, Mother's reclusiveness deepened. Dad more and more engaged in business and later in the politics of local education, Mother more and more chose to stay at home.

Already outsiders, by virtue of being Catholic in a predominantly Lutheran town without a Catholic church, my parents had few settings in which to interact socially with the community. Mother probably never dreamed she would end up a housewife in a rural community. She had trained to be a teacher and treasured the cultural opportunities afforded by a college education and a larger community.

Briefly she participated in the Mid-Century Club, a woman's organization featuring weekly luncheon meetings and programs put on by the members. But, when one program required that she don a mustache, wear a white blouse and sing barbershop tunes as part of a quartet, she quit.

"I can't do it!" she cried in a rare display of emotion in our house. "I don't want to do it," she said for emphasis. "I have nothing in common with those women."

Over the years, she rarely mentioned having any difficulties. But once, in a letter to me as an adult, she acknowledged having a problem with depression. So rare was such an admission that I quickly flew to State College, Pennsylvania, where she and Dad and my sisters lived at the time, to learn more.

Sue, Eileen and I gathered with Dad in a coffee shop to talk about Mother's health. She complained, not only of depression, but also of pervasive, intense lower back pain. Medication prescribed for both conditions had not helped. My understanding was that medication for depression often does not help if the person involved has *reason* to be depressed.

"Dad, how are you holding up?" I asked him as he slumped forward in his chair.

"It's tough. I don't know what to do," he said. "Mother needs help, but nothing seems to be working."

"And you, how are *you* doing?" I asked again, placing my hand on his arm. At that, he broke down and cried.

"You girls are a great comfort," he mumbled, head down, trying to regain his composure.

Another time, when I was sitting with Mother and drinking coffee, she raised the topic of the fear she experienced in leaving the house.

"I believe I have agoraphobia," she said. "I've read about it and it sounds like me."

The self-diagnosis fit. My mother avoided crowds and left the house only with a specific purpose in mind—going to the grocery store, visiting the library, or going out to eat at one of the several buffet restaurants. Yet I wondered if what she described was more a case of intense shyness and loneliness.

Fortunately, Mother's love of reading and music, not to mention the always-present dog on her lap, saved her from despair and gave her life meaning and direction. During my visits, we frequently sat together and shared what we were listening to and reading.

"Diane, I've made a tape of my favorite music from the radio," she brightened as she handed me a cassette tape with handwritten notes on the titles and composers.

"Who is your favorite?" I asked, wishing to expand my own knowledge of classical music.

"I love Liszt and particularly his Consolation 3 in D Major," she replied. "Do you know it?

We listened to it together and I imagined learning how to play the piece on the piano.

"Mother, I'd love to play it someday."

Our conversations continued as she shared other things she was doing—compiling an extensive list of words for working crossword puzzles and playing a beloved organ that gave her hours of pleasure. Her letters spoke of frequent trips to the library with my sisters and shopping trips with her sister Anne, who had moved to join the family in Pennsylvania.

Yet, I felt a rush of sadness for her life and the lives of other women who sacrificed dreams in the interests of fulfilling the roles expected of them. On the other hand, I know Mother found satisfying pursuits to enrich her time. But I wonder how it was especially for her, but also for my dad and for their life together, when I was born.

It was 1946, one year after Dad returned from fighting in Germany on the front lines of World War II. Having witnessed death and violence, he, like so many other men and women, came back to the United States seeking a normal life away from the fear and trauma that characterized the battlefield. He and Mother wanted to resume their life together and restart a marriage only six years old. Like millions of others, they wanted to have another baby.

During that post-war period, millions of babies were born—babies who would grow up to be the boomers and dominate American culture for half a century. I was one of those babies, but from the moment of birth, it was clear I was different, potentially fatally different. My spinal cord protruded through a membrane-covered sac on my lower back.

"Here's your baby," the doctor said to my mother as he thrust me into her arms. "She won't live long with this opening in her spine."

Still absorbing this shocking news, my mother choked out, "Will she ever go to school?"

"If she lives, maybe. But she's not likely to walk," he said.

When I asked my dad about those early days, all he said was, "They didn't give us much hope." His eyes, glistening with tears, gave away the depth of his emotion.

In the 1940s and 1950s, some doctors advised

not treating babies like me, anticipating what they called a "low quality of life." That's what my attending physician recommended. "She won't last long. Keep her comfortable and try not to get too attached."

My parents returned home, baptized me a few days later, and then waited for my death. Raised Roman Catholic, they believed what they had been taught—that a baby who died before being baptized would not go to heaven, but rather to Limbo, a place between Heaven and Hell, a sort of parking spot for people who did not belong either place.

In those early days and weeks, treating me like a fragile, breakable doll, my parents puzzled over how to hold me, how to place me in a crib, and whether to risk getting too attached to me. To avoid breaking the sac, which was made of a smooth, tough skin that encased the spinal cord on my back, and to prevent introducing an infection, they laid me on my stomach. They held me gingerly, one hand on my bottom and the other on my upper back and diapered me carefully, laying me on my side to minimize pressure on that sac.

Is it an actual memory or a dream, an event that happened once or something that happened often? I'll never know. But this is my memory: I am lying in my crib. The room is dark. I hear voices and footsteps. My mother. My big sister. I cry out hoping to be picked up. They come close to my door. I cry again. They pass by. The voices fade away.

Was I medicated for pain? Comforted? Admired? Shown to the relatives? The questions were too painful to ask my parents while they were still alive. Now I can only imagine what they did and said at the time: Dad telephoning his parents and my aunts and uncles explaining in hushed tones that my life was expected to be short. My mother crying, perhaps feeling shame or inadequacy for having a less than perfect baby. Eileen, five years of age at my birth, peeking into my room, asking to hold me and being told, "Not now, honey, maybe later."

Would there be a later? Would I be around in a week, a month or longer? Should they allow their first-born to draw close to a baby destined to die?

Dad and Mother had come through the war, bought a little house in Waterloo, Iowa, and became pregnant with me, fulfilling their dreams. And now those dreams dissipated before their eyes. When I was six months old, Mother was already expecting another baby. Becoming pregnant again soon after my birth may have reflected my parents' anticipation of my death. Or their desire for a normal, healthy child. Or both.

Mother cared for Eileen and me as best she could and prepared for the arrival of another baby. She made our clothes, prepared meals and looked after us until Dad came home later in the evening. Unlike many families during that era, her parents and siblings lived too far away to be of daily help.

Within months, despite predictions, I wanted to crawl, join family activities and cuddle. My parents never trusted anyone else with my care, but once, when both my parents had the flu, I went to stay with my grandparents.

"You were such a good baby," Grandma recalled. "You never cried."

A photo from the time shows Dad holding me—an alert, apparently healthy baby about six months old, smartly dressed in a soft cotton flair coat with ball trim along the cuffs and a matching cap. I did not appear destined to die anytime soon. Dad smiled proudly in the photo.

Amazed and surprised by my resilience, my parents began to ask new questions of their local physician. "Were the doctors wrong?" "Will she live? "Will she be able to walk?" "What are we supposed to do now?"

Their questions eventually led them to The University of Iowa Hospitals and Clinic in the spring of 1948, where a surgeon agreed to see me. Without hesitation, he recommended surgery to close the opening on my back. My parents hoped this operation would make their little girl normal, but, alas, the surgeon was not able to fix all the problems spina bifida caused to the organs in my lower body. I was unable to control my bladder. One of my kidneys did not function.

My parents catheterized me as instructed by the doctor, inserting a slim rubber tube through the urethra into the bladder, but an hour later I dribbled urine again, requiring the continual wearing of a diaper. My parents set about doing this with little help or guidance, except for what they received at the time of my surgery.

At first my mother tended to my needs, but gradually my father took over. My mother may have been reluctant to carry out this procedure. More likely, my father, obsessively concerned about cleanliness, believed he was better equipped to attend to the details of the procedure. He was determined to avoid the ever-present threat of an infection in my bladder that could threaten my remaining kidney. Their dedication meant that throughout childhood, I did not have a single urinary tract infection.

My family planned their schedule around this ritual of catheterization. Whether we stayed at home or traveled, they catheterized me before breakfast, after lunch and dinner, and before bedtime. Four times a day, my dad boiled water on our kitchen gas stove in a small white lacquer pan, added the catheter, and boiled and sterilized it for about five minutes.

Then he called out, "Diane, I'm ready." I ran to a bedroom, stretched out on the bed so that my bottom was near the end, and then he pulled off the diaper I always wore in case of leakage. Dad washed the area around the urethra with soap and water, using a fresh cloth and towel each time. Then he coated the end of the catheter with K-Y jelly and inserted it into my urethra and up into the bladder. The slit in the tip of the catheter allowed the urine to empty into another pan.

The procedure didn't hurt, usually, and it was a relief to hear the urine draining into the pan, especially if my bladder was full. Then my dad refastened the diaper, setting me free again. I complied without complaint, not a surprise since this was the way I had gone to the bathroom every day since infancy. The fact that everyone else did it differently underscored the fact I was unique. Still, I was curious and asked Susie, my younger sister, who remarkably remembered, to explain how it worked for her.

"Mother or Dad would tell me to go to the bathroom and sit on the stool," she said.

"How old were you when you started doing this?" I asked.

"About two or three. They didn't tell me how to go. They just turned on the water and asked me to try," she continued. "Eventually I learned how."

"That's it? It sounds so simple," I said with some envy. "And then you stopped wearing a diaper?"

Susie nodded and, unprompted, responded to the question she sensed was on my mind.

"We knew you were different. You needed extra help. That was just the way it was," her casual tone suggesting this was not a big deal.

In spite of this, somewhere along the way I gathered that my situation, more specifically my body, was something to be embarrassed about. The absence of any explanation for or discussion about my situation puzzled me. Did being "different from" somehow mean "less than"? At some level, I sensed this was the case.

Yet, for all intents and purposes, life at the Cox home looked like life in any of the small houses in any of the small towns in the Midwest.

During the 1950s and 1960s, schools with 15 to 20 students per class joined with other districts to increase their economic feasibility. In this era of school reorganization, a proposal to merge the Arlington school district with Oelwein, twenty miles away, gained momentum. That would have required students to ride the bus one to two hours a day.

"That's too long," Dad said. "I don't want the girls on the bus that much every day." He may have been thinking about my limitations. How would I manage an unpredictable bladder that far away?

His concern led to activism, a fact I am proud of to this day. He came up with his own idea— merge Arlington with Strawberry Point and Lamont, two other small towns. Put the high school in the middle of all three so that no town would be more than five miles away from the school.

The idea took root and before long he was running for the school board, preparing for a bond issue, campaigning first for his election, and, once on the board, for service as its chairman. This man, with his high school education, smelling of hog dust and lacking connections with the movers and shakers, nonetheless brought about a significant, lasting change in the lives of thousands of people over the decades. A plaque recognizing the contributions of this founding board still resides in the entry of Starmont Schools.

When we talked in our family, we talked about perfunctory, obvious things. When one person said something, another responded briefly. Often, family members said nothing at all.

"I need to buy groceries today," Mother said to Dad. "Can I have fifteen dollars?"

"Girls, we're going over to Elkader for hamburgers," Dad announced to our cheers.

"It's time to go to Confession," Mother said. "We'll stop at the Kohl's afterward to look for shoes for you and Susie."

"Can we have strawberry sodas tonight?" either Susie or I asked in the heat of summer days.

I know from talking with friends that certain interactions occurring in other homes rarely took place in ours, exchanges that might have started with questions like these:

"Girls, what did you learn in school today?"

"How are your piano lessons going, Diane?"

"What are you planning for the spring concert at school?"

"That's great, Eileen. Homecoming Queen. How did that feel?"

"You look a little sad, Susie. What's going on?"

"What would you like to do this summer?"

"You're looking especially pretty today, Diane! What's different?"

The fact that a comment my grandfather made one day sticks so vividly in my mind attests to how hungry I was for feedback, particularly about my appearance.

Someone raised a question about me in my presence at my grandparents' house in Volga after Sunday Mass. I do not recall the question and it doesn't matter. What matters is that my grandfather, usually an angry, opinionated man who dominated any occasion at which he was present, praised me.

"I don't know about that, but I do know Diane is sure a pretty girl," he said.

No discussion followed. No one agreed with his assessment. I probably blushed and looked away. But, at age twelve, at the onset of adolescence, I reveled in those magic words, "Diane is sure a pretty girl."

In junior high, after working for months on the piano piece, "Bolero," for a music competition, I told Mother and Dad that I was going to participate and they quickly said, "Oh, that's not necessary. You don't have to compete."

I didn't protest or even ask why. Much to my teacher's disappointment, I informed her I would not be going.

My parents might have been concerned about my bladder giving out or uncertain how and when to catheterize me before and after the contest. They might have been uncomfortable attending the competition themselves if that was expected. Or they might have wanted to downplay the importance of my competing. I was already a student who loved academic competition and earned an A in every subject.

I'll never know because we never talked about it.

But to their credit, they encouraged my curiosity about the world. When the local library lacked the information I needed to complete a badge for Girl Scouts, Mother and Dad drove me to Waterloo to use the city's larger facility. My Christmas presents were as likely to be books on geology and astronomy and science kits, as pajamas and toys. What they shied away from was any involvement that took them out into the public, along with their children.

Susie remembers asking Mother to attend one of her basketball games since neither parent had seen her play. Mother did come, Susie, said, but she said nothing afterward, no comments about the team or about Susie's performance. Susie told me later in life that Mother may have been trying to be diplomatic since Susie's performance was so bad the coach encouraged her to pursue other school activities.

While our parents did not always attend their children's activities in the community, neither were they unkind. I do not ever recall any comment that hurt my feelings or felt unwarranted. Mother and Dad were gentle with us and with the friends we brought home from school. To this day at class reunions, these friends talk about how much they liked my parents.

"Do you remember the afternoon we sneaked through the back door of the school and dashed across the street to your house when your mother was making brownies?" my classmate Diane asked me years later when we were well into adulthood.

Actually, I didn't remember.

"The principal was waiting for us at the back door when we returned," she continued.

"'Where have you girls been?' he asked. His words were stern, but he repressed a smile. We were hardly the school's troublemakers.

"Your dad always went with us when we trick-or-treated," Becky recalled at a lunch we set up to reminisce about our childhood. "And when your dad spoke, we always listened."

"Wasn't it wonderful to have good parents when we were kids?" another friend Janice said at a class reunion. Susie recalls the same thing.

"Every one of our friends liked Mother and Dad," she said.

Apparently, Mother and Dad parented in much the same way they had been raised. They spoke when the need called for it but rarely expressed how they felt. One day, out of the blue, my mother said, "The only time my parents praised me was when my mother said, 'You've raised a good family, Helen.'"

While my dad's father spoke mainly to criticize or reprimand, his mother was funny and warm. Sitting in her lap one day as a little girl, I pointed to one of her breasts and said, "What's that, Grandma?"

"Oh, Grandma ate too much," she said and laughed so hard she cried, dabbing her eyes with a lace-edged floral handkerchief.

When our visits to Dad's parents stretched through late afternoon and into the evening hours, I would crawl into his lap, a thumb in my mouth, and with a little finger stroke the soft undershirt he wore.

"It tickled," Dad admitted much later in life, "but I didn't want to say anything."

I remember one day when Eileen, Susie and I were sitting at the kitchen table of my mother's mother, Grandma Popchuck. They were chattering away about something when Grandma turned and said to me, "Why do you not talk?"

Why **didn't** I talk? I wondered, as this Russian full-bodied woman in a loose-fitting floral dress went on with her work, kneading a huge mound of dark bread dough and sighing, "… such a quiet one." I wonder now why I *was* so quiet. No one ever told me to be quiet, but I had learned by example that some things were better not shared. If I started chatting, something might slip out, my secret would be exposed and I would embarrass myself. I held on to that lesson for the rest of my life.

So, my compliance—and my silence—in regard to catheterization became a given. It is remarkable to me now, but for thirteen years, I acquiesced to my father conducting this procedure without complaint. But one particularly painful episode shifted my view.

On a rare road trip, my family and I visited Mother's sister's house in Denver for a few days' stay. Aunt Teckia could spare a bedroom for my parents, but we girls needed to use the sofa in the living room, as well as blankets she spread out on the floor. We stepped over one another over the course of several days as we each woke up at different times in the night.

One day during our visit, as Dad catheterized me in the bedroom my aunt designated for my parents, someone—an aunt, uncle or cousin, I don't remember who—walked into the room as I was lying there, my legs spread, a tube running from my bladder.

"Oh, excuse me!" the person said.

"It's okay," Dad replied. "Diane doesn't mind."

"Diane doesn't mind?" Dad assumed he knew how I felt. He no longer considered the sight of my genital area a big deal. It was readily available when I needed to empty my bladder. Couldn't he have pulled a cover over my legs? Instructed the intruder to come back in ten or fifteen minutes?

During this exchange, I stared at the wallpaper in the room, attempting to erase the distress on my face and pull back the cry in my throat. Red roses, small green leaves, lacy edging. Who picked this wallpaper? How long had it been up? Did I like it?

My private parts, no longer something special to Dad, were no longer special to me. Or, so he concluded. I stared out the window to the backyard. A bird feeder swaying in the breeze. Is that a finch? I watched her fly effortlessly into the sky. I wanted to be that finch right now and fly away.

Granted, I had long ago surrendered control over the emptying of my bladder. Yet at that moment I realized that the privacy I had taken for granted, this most intimate act of catheterization, was not private at all. My body was available for viewing at will.

Wood beams ran the length of the ceiling. I counted the beams. One, two, three, four. The woodwork and framed windows matched the wood of the beams. Wallpaper, birds, woodwork. I struggled to stay present when all I wanted to do was to escape.

My tightened throat could not release words. I could have gasped "Mine!" and grabbed a blanket. Or objected, "Dad, no!" and waved away the intruder. I could have cried after it was all over. But that meant rejecting the rules I unknowingly had agreed to during a time of innocence and dependency. Dad still thought of me as that child he took care of in infancy. But I was no infant, I was no child. I was a pre-adolescent with a dawning sense that this was no longer right.

Glancing out the window, I imagined myself again to be that bird, free to fly away, free to be somewhere else, free to be someone else. Anyone else.

At various stages of my life, I heard the same question:

"Why do you not talk more?" a college professor asked, recommending I read *Silences* by Tillie Olson.

To talk is to assert you have something valuable to say, that others will be interested, that you are worthy to take up space and time. Talking opens up conversation, conversation that could go anywhere. In defined situations like classrooms where the assignment was clear, I performed appropriately and spoke, sometimes articulately, but in everyday life I shied away from intimate conversations and withdrew from many situations.

This reticence was a problem that continued through most of my life. When we have people over to dinner and I say something, if no one asks a follow-up question or if I don't discern interest on their faces, I stop talking. As a relatively high-functioning adult, I struggle to speak my thoughts and feelings if not encouraged by others with smiles or head nods.

"What's the series of portraits on your wall?" our dinner guest asked one night. Six of us had gathered around the table at our condo in Des Moines—our neighbors across the hall and an older couple with whom we had developed a friendship. The conversation up until then had been lively, with one neighbor having told the story of growing up in rural Iowa, largely in response to my genuine interest and questioning.

"Oh, they're Bedouin women," I responded casually.

He said nothing. I assumed he had little interest in knowing more, so I said nothing.

In retrospect, I realize fear stopped me. Fear I would not be able to tell the story behind the portraits. Fear no one would care. Fear my voice would falter.

Yet, the story was worth relating. I had traveled to Tunisia on an exchange program helping local women start and expand businesses. One afternoon, another Des Moines woman and I took off for the Old City in Tunis to go shopping. At an antique shop, I found these portraits, old postcards in sepia tones of four young women in robes and headdress, one woman holding a baby on her back. On impulse, I bought them and have loved them ever since.

Our adventure that day included exploring the

inner pathways of the ancient marketplace with the goal of purchasing a rug. When a man in the market offered to direct my friend and me to a reputable rug merchant, we followed him without hesitation.

"You did what?" my host, the Tunisian woman of the family with whom I was staying, said later after I described our adventure and my successful purchase of a brightly colored turquoise and red patterned rug to be shipped back to Iowa. She was horrified at my recklessness. "And you gave him your credit card?" she said. At that, she called her husband into the room.

"Do you realize how risky that behavior was?" he said after being briefed on my transgression. "Why wouldn't you ask us to take you and guide you? That rug you bought—chances are you will never see it," he continued.

The story, told well, could have entertained those gathered around our dinner table. I could have shown them the rug that had arrived in the small Carlisle post office years earlier or discussed the entertaining scene at the rug merchant's store with young men streaming out from everywhere with chai tea on trays and new rugs for me to examine.

But, I said nothing.

Another time, as a member of a women's study club, I not only hosted a luncheon in our home, I prepared a paper for presentation, one I had worked on for months. This paper required researching and writing about two of my favorite topics—Iowa women and Ragtime music. Following the presentation of the paper, I planned to play a ragtime composition on the piano.

I was excited about my speech, but as the guests began to arrive, I could feel my throat tightening up. I began whispering my greetings, trying to save my vocal chords. But by the time of the presentation, I had lost my voice entirely. Reluctantly, I asked my friend to read the paper, which was later published in a revised format in *The Iowan*. I sat listening to her, disappointed that she, not I, was presenting it. Beyond that, I was frustrated with my voice for failing me. This was my opportunity to speak my own words, my own creative effort. Was fear shutting me down?

I followed the speech with my piano performance. Sitting at the keyboard, my fingers poised above the black and white keys, I felt calm for the first time that day. No words were expected of me—just the sounds of my fingers dancing over the keys.

The breast cancer community taught me to share in a more honest and intimate way— how I felt about this diagnosis, what was happening to my body in treatment, and concerns and fears about the future. Friends and family listened compassionately when I cried in dread of chemotherapy. My oncologist assured me I was "tough," strong enough to get through this, as he gave me a hug.

People *did* care about what I thought, so I had every reason to believe others would listen with empathy if I talked about the toll spina bifida had taken on me. And yet I remained silent.

Tillie Olsen wrote in *Silences*, "The silences I speak of here are unnatural: the unnatural thwarting of what struggles to come into being, but cannot."

Her words resonated deeply with me. At this point in my life, I wanted to be truthful. I wanted to be whole. Regardless of whether I was cured or not, I wanted to be healed. Not a breast, not a bladder, but a body, a whole person living with integrity. Such integrity would require looking at and talking about the "secrets" in my life, the shame I felt over my body, the lack of worthiness. I knew my story was bigger than breast cancer, even bigger than spina bifida. It was about secrecy—how it begins, how it impedes us, and how it takes a toll on our lives. My story was about finding new footing, new confidence, new voice.

And so, in the year after my breast cancer diagnosis, I set about experimenting with a new choreography for my life—a new rhythm, new pace, new steps, new focus. The inner music I had danced to throughout my life slowed and became more intentional. No longer interested in my high-stress job as the public relations and marketing voice of the newspaper, I resigned (two years before early retirement benefits would have been available) and opened a new file on my computer desktop titled, "My Life."

4
OPENING THE ENVELOPE

Pam Reese, the University of Iowa's Hardin Medical Library librarian, said, "I didn't know what to expect," after meeting me for the first time. "Would you be able to walk? Would you be in a wheelchair?"

I stared at her for a moment, not understanding why she would say such a thing.

Noticing my discomfort, she stumbled, "I'm sorry...."

Finally, it dawned on me why she would wonder. Of course. The only thing she knew about me was that I had spina bifida. Then I realized how deep my secret had been. Rarely had I met someone aside from doctors who knew I had spina bifida. She expected me to have a visible physical disability of some kind.

I quickly reassured her. "Oh, that's okay. I've been lucky. Most people with spina bifida do have difficulty walking, but I'm fine in that regard."

I was 54, three years after my diagnosis with breast cancer in 1999, and on a quest to find out about my body. About myself. About the decisions my parents faced when I was an infant with an open spine.

Cradling a notebook, a pillow to cushion my lower back, and a latte, I turned to Pam for direction on where to go.

"You'll need to finish that coffee first," she said. "We're always concerned about protecting our materials."

"Of course," I responded, taking a few more quick sips and then handing it to her for disposal.

"I've pulled some materials for you on spina bifida. We'll go to the lower area of the library," she said, gesturing to the stairs. "You can take them okay?"

"Yes, I'm fine," I said again. Her considerate attention brought up an old mental script. "Don't talk about this and no one will notice. Don't make an issue of it. Don't draw attention to yourself. You can handle this."

Pushing aside these thoughts, I followed Pam down into a large room filled with oak tables worn from years of use. Shelves of hundreds of medical journals reached back into the dark recesses of an adjoining room. A narrow band of windows around the perimeter permitted limited sunlight to enter. The chairs were empty. Students and medical researchers were elsewhere, at least for that day, likely more interested in reading current research and futuristic thinking than going through outdated information. The mustiness and subdued lighting of the room comforted me. I wanted to go back, even if that meant descending for a time into the darkness of the reality of what my parents and I struggled with in the post-WWII era.

Pam had set up a workstation for me, piled with the articles from the list I sent a couple of weeks earlier. She added other relevant books and periodicals. Many of the publications had not been checked out for over thirty years.

Some of the books contained basic information about spina bifida. They defined spina bifida as any congenital defect involving insufficient closure of the spine, occurring once in every 1000 live births. The rate of occurrence varied by demographic group. In 75 percent of those cases, the spinal cord and membranes covering the spinal cord protrude out the back, resulting in what's known as a myelomeningocele.

Where the opening occurs determines the severity of the neurological damage. The higher the opening and the protrusion of the spinal cord, the greater the loss of function in the lower body. Symptoms include partial or complete paralysis of the legs and often loss of bladder control. The exposed spinal cord is susceptible to infection— even meningitis.

I continued to read the information about all

the ways that spina bifida can happen and how it affects those born with it. As I read, I realized how lucky I was that my opening was low in the sacral area, affecting primarily bladder function.

This opportunity for in-depth research started with a decision three months earlier to ask for my medical records from the University of Iowa. My family doctor assured me such records were not kept that far back, but with little to lose, I completed a medical request form on the University's website.

A few weeks later on a sunny May day, shortly after lunch, the postman delivered a plain brown envelope along with the usual assortment of bills, solicitations, magazines and credit card offers. Retrieving the large envelope from the mailbox, I immediately spotted the return address, the University of Iowa Hospitals. My address was hand-written, lending a personal touch to an official communication. Some generous person had retrieved information more than 50 years old from microfiche records, probably in remote storage facilities.

With a sharp intake of air and a rapid heart-beat, I sat down at the oak table in the sun room of our home and paused to reflect. Did I really want to know about those early events in 1947, when my life hung in the balance? Yes, of course. Understanding what my parents faced, what I faced, was my mission. With trepidation, I gently pried open the envelope.

Inside were thirteen pages of single-spaced data—an initial assessment by the attending surgeon, an operation record, pathology report, letters to a local family physician, and follow-up reports taking me through the second year of my life. Prepared on a manual typewriter, the paper streaked with copier marks, the type fuzzy, and the margins filled with handwritten notes, these reports nonetheless provided a clear picture of my health and prognosis in those first months of life.

"This baby was a full-term child," the report read. "The mother asserts she was well throughout the pregnancy. Baby seemed to be well in all respects at birth except for a mass in the low sacral region... the mass is now as large as a tangerine. Advise: Surgical removal."

Some concerns were immediate, even before surgery. Additional tests showed my left kidney no longer worked and infection from a neurogenic bladder, a bladder that didn't empty properly because of damage to the nervous system, flooded my body. In response, a nurse emptied my bladder with a catheter, a procedure my parents learned that day and continued, and she began to treat me with antibiotics.

Surgery followed. According to the report, Dr.

Russell Meyers, chair of the Division of Neuro-surgery at The University of Iowa, opened the sac on my lower back, freed the sacral spinal cord, placed it back in the canal, and closed the open-ing with silk sutures. In cases like mine, with an open spine, meningitis represented a real and potentially lethal threat. The subsequent report identified the procedure as "excision and repair of myelomeningocele."

"Only time will tell how much neurological dysfunction will be permanent," Dr. Meyers said in a follow-up letter to my parents.

My parents brought me home, tended to the surgical wound until it healed, and then they relaxed a bit, feeling free to hold me and to let me play on the floor. Soon I was pulling myself up on the coffee table in the living room, taking tiny, tentative steps, falling, getting up and try-ing again. Swaying to the music playing on the radio, I lifted one foot and then the other, trying to dance. Before long, I was running around the house and playing like an almost normal child.

The report held no surprises—until I looked at the date—May of 1948. Dr. Meyers did not see me until nine months after my birth. Nine months? That was a long time to have an open spine, a long time to live in a crib, a long time to be picked up and carried gingerly, a long time to be kept from casual play, I thought. At that mo-ment a conversation with my mother, years ago, long before I knew anything about the timing of my treatment, came to mind.

"Dr. Meyers was angry," she said.

"Angry at what?" I asked, speculating what his response might have meant. Was he angry at the local doctor who advised against treatment? At my parents who had not acted more quickly? Or at the fact that other babies with spina bifida were left to die?

Mother slumped in her chair, pulled her shoulders inward and looked down, saying nothing more.

"It's okay, Mother," I reassured her, draping an arm around her and sitting close, not wanting to cause her any further regrets about the past.

Research at the Hardin Library showed I had defied the odds. In a day-long search through periodicals and journals, I found a study of cases approximating my situation:

Research at the Department of Paediatrics at the United Oxford Hospitals by Hide, Williams and Ellis found that between January 1, 1958 and December 31, 1968, 92 of 99 infants with myelomeningocele who, like me, were not treated at birth, died within the first year—9 within 24 hours, an additional 56 within three months and another 27 by one year. Only four children reached their second birthday, and only two children remained alive at the end of the study.

While impossible to know, of course, whether I would have been like those two children who survived or if, more likely, I would have died before my first birthday as so many did, I suspect my surgery at 10 months saved my life. But, Dr. Meyers did caution in the medical report, "The prognosis is still rather guarded in cases like this."

Journal articles in the Hardin Library reiterated that infanticide was firmly rejected in cases of babies born with open spines in the era in which I was born. Doctors sometimes delayed surgery to see if hydrocephalus or fluid collection in the brain developed, which occurred in about 90 percent of cases of myelomeningocele. (I was fortunate not to have this complication.) In the 1940s, the baby would likely die if this happened since shunt systems or brain drains would not be in use until the 1950s.

In some cases, doctors rejected surgery as unmerited or unlikely to be successful. Or they feared that by performing surgery and prolonging life, they were placing an unreasonable burden on the family to care for children with severe developmental problems. Even if surgery saved the child's life, the parents and the child might face subsequent lifelong distress and misery, according to this view. As evidenced in journal articles, doctors actively debated these questions at professional conferences, and they sponsored studies seeking answers. To my everlasting gratitude, Dr. Meyers had no reservations about treatment. I had the surgery. I survived.

Thanking Pam for her help, leaving the subdued recesses of the library, and emerging
from the library, I entered a brilliantly sunny May
day. As my eyes adjusted to the light, I took in
the stretch of green lawn, unfurling upward like
a spool of ribbon, inviting me to the campus life
that shimmered around me. Students strolled
from one dignified stone building to another,
softening the formality of their surroundings
with their casual attire—jeans and t-shirts.

I imagined their banter—talking, laughing,
and planning weekend excursions and gatherings. They were there to study, but as important-
ly, they were there to learn about themselves and
one another.

Thoughts floated through my head, much as
the clouds above formed and broke apart in the
sky. My study of the past yielded insights about
the present. Now the present challenged me to
engage with life in a new way. A plane soared
overhead, slicing through a sky so blue I wanted
to wrap it around me.

What struck me most of all was the light. Light
reflecting off newly emerged leaves, light bouncing off white stone, light beaming from student
faces, light casting deep shadows and accenting

green grass. The scene came to me as a gift, reminding me that my life itself was a gift.

Just moments before, the past had enshrouded me—the pain, the despair, the doubt, and the uncertainties doctors, parents, and patients endured in those days before medical knowledge provided clear direction. But now I realized how fortunate I was to be alive, diagnoses or prognoses no longer defining me as someone limited or flawed. By some miracle, I had survived spina bifida and now breast cancer. It was time to put away the articles I had copied and the notes I had taken that day. It was time to release the questions that prompted my research. I had answered them to my satisfaction.

Now it was time to be happy. I could walk fast, striding to the parking ramp, or I could linger. I chose to dawdle, sitting on a nearby rock and putting down my canvas bag to look at the flowers, impatiens now visited by spit-fire hummingbirds back from Costa Rica and those stargazer lilies pinker than any lipstick I wear. They were the flowers in my wedding bouquet when Jeff and I married.

Then dancing along the sidewalk to the parking ramp, I said thank you to the wind, to anyone passing by, to God, to this world opening up to me in a surprising new way. Thank you to Mother and Dad for not giving up, to doctors for applying their skill in the absence of solid research, for teachers who nurtured my creativity and curiosity, for sisters who befriended me for life, for my loving husband, and now for the friends who walked with me not only through breast cancer, but also for whatever might lie ahead.

At that moment in time and space, everything was right, no waiting, no rationalizing, no antici-pating, no thinking. I let the grace of my life fall upon me, taking it into my cells, breathing it into my lungs, and holding it deep in my heart. Life had blessed me.

A Note of Grace

My parents had few resources during my childhood, and, because of their reticent nature, they seldom reached out for help. Nonetheless, a note of grace attached itself to my family's life, bringing a sometimes unexpected, yet welcome turn of events. Anne, the older sister of my mother, and by personality the more dominant of the two, took action in cases where Mother and Dad were confused, afraid or paralyzed by uncertainty.

So when it became apparent, in my adult years, that now *she* was the vulnerable one, that *she* needed someone to get involved in her life, I felt a special responsibility to be that someone.

In the mid-1990's, the bank called alerting my sisters and me that someone named Tom was attempting to withdraw her money with a check she had signed. With a police record, Tom was not the sort of person we wanted befriending our now 87-year-old aunt. Longing to feel needed again, she had fallen for this man more than forty years her junior. And she had literally fall-en—on the steps of her apartment building. The manager of her low-income apartment building called to say she feared for Anne's safety after she discovered her on the front steps of the com-plex, bleeding and incoherent. After talking with Eileen and Sue, I announced to Jeff that I was leaving for Pennsylvania to help her.

Jeff sighed, fearing, I suspect, that I was rush-ing off on another of my impulsive missions. He started to respond, then stopped, and finally said, "But what will you do?"

"Whatever it takes," I said. "Move her to an as-sisted living place or some other facility where she will be well cared for, clear out her apartment, find her the medical attention she needs...." I had no idea how to do this, but it was clear this job was mine. Get there, I reasoned, and figure out later what steps to take to save her from this predator.

I looked at Jeff, wanting some response. I wait-ed. Finally, always concerned about my safety, he said, "I'm going with you."

When we flew from Des Moines to State Col-lege and arrived unannounced, would she let us in? When we sized up the situation, and when we came up with a solution, would Aunt Anne be receptive or resistant? When we met Tom, would he threaten either her or us, or would he leave easily? Without answers, we flew to State College.

When we opened the door of Aunt Anne's apartment, the sight of broken glass concerned us, and the smell of rotting food staggered us. I fell back a step or two into the hallway, not sure whether I wanted to go in. Then we saw her, slumped in her chair.

"Careful," Jeff whispered as we made our way through discarded clothes, shards of glass and garbage.

"Hello, Anne," I said softly, approaching her chair and crouching at eye level. "We just happened to be in the area and decided to stop in."

Disoriented, Anne looked up and said nothing. Then, she recognized me. "Diane! Is that you?"

"We're here to help you," I responded. Jeff approached and gently took her frail, liver-spotted hand.

"What do you mean?" she asked.

"It's time to move and find a new place for you to live," I ventured with some trepidation, anticipating her response.

"I can't move. Tom needs me. How will he find me?" she said, words now stumbling out of her mouth as her eyes wandered around the apartment. "He has cancer and no money for treatment. I told him I would help. I have a check for him somewhere."

Jeff touched my arm to offer reassurance as I searched for words to describe our plan. "Aunt Anne, you can't live here anymore," I said. "Tom can take care of himself. It's time to leave."

Amazingly, she didn't resist, in a manner completely unlike the person I had known since childhood. The woman who single-handedly set up a meal site for the homeless in the neighborhood by providing microwaved frozen dinners in the lobby of her apartment building, that is until the manager shut her down. The woman who moved her brother's dead body to a new grave over the objections of his wife. The woman who had given my sisters and me plenty of grief over the years through her increasing demands for personal attention and special treatment in light of "all I have done for you." Anne was no lavender lady in lace. So I took her lack of protest as a sign of her rapidly deteriorating mental and physical health.

With the goal of relocating Aunt Anne as quickly as possible, I tried my best to sound confident. But later that night, before we started the move, I wavered. "Jeff, I don't know if we can do this. Her apartment is a disaster. Tom is a menace." By then I was crying.

"Talk it over with Eileen. Perhaps she'll have some suggestions," he said.

So I called her. Eileen, my big sister who lived in Texas, was someone I could always go to for help. Well-grounded and a master of logistics, she could be counted on to outline a practical plan.

"We'll come to help you," she offered. "Larry is ready to go." Larry, her husband and my brother-in-law, affirmed that offer by calling out in the background of our phone conversation his willingness to make the trip from Texas. Just knowing we could call on either of them calmed me.

"No, let's wait and see," I said. "I feel better after talking with you. Jeff and I will tackle this and keep you posted on our progress."

In the next few days, we hauled out the trash, swept up the broken glass, and emptied out the refrigerator. With Eileen's help (working by phone from her home in Texas), we worked through the mountain of details of her life—discontinuing utilities, filling out the paperwork associated with her application for Medicaid and trying to make sense of her financial records.

My body ached as we cleaned out the apartment. Oh, for a glass of wine and a swim in the hotel pool to find some relief for my lower back and legs. But Anne had settled into her new place, and we wanted to help her adjust. Driving the two blocks to the nursing home, we found her in the home's lounge reading the newspaper, chatting with the aides, and looking altogether relaxed.

Back in her private room, she opened with glee the packages I brought—new slippers, a pink nightgown and matching robe, and a plush sweater to take off the chill. I pulled out the family photo album and began to leaf through it.

"Remember the time you took us to St. Louis to see *Brigadoon* in an outdoor amphitheater and it rained right up to the minute the performance was to start?" I asked, recalling one of my favorite childhood memories spent with Susie, Mother, and Anne. "That was a magical evening, seeing the rain stop, the lights come on and the actors and actresses emerge."

That got her started, and we talked about our mutual love for music and the series of musicals we had seen together in Des Moines, Chicago, and New York.

"Oooh, I loved seeing Yul Brenner in *The King and I* when we went to Chicago. Is he still alive? He can put his bedroom slippers under my bed anytime," Anne chortled, warming up to this idea of recalling past musical adventures.

"Well, if we're going to talk swooning, I'd choose Robert Goulet in *Camelot*. When he sang 'If ever I would leave you,' I thought, 'No chance you're leaving *me*,'" I responded, giggling. Jeff's face lightened with amusement.

"Anne, do you want to keep your cassette tapes in your room or should we give them to the library here in the building?" I inquired.

"Oh, let's donate them to the library so others can enjoy them." Anne was beginning to relax, or so it seemed.

Jeff took pictures of Anne and me sitting on her bed, both of us with big smiles. We hung a favorite Georgia O'Keeffe poster Anne and I purchased together at The Institute of Art in Chicago. The picture, fluffy white clouds on a blue background, hovered high above the room, giving a sense of airiness to her space.

Back at her apartment, we continued to sort through the chaos that was her life, a process that would take days. I found her birth certificate in a pile of trash under her bed and her Power of Attorney, designating Eileen, Susie, and me, in a cupboard with cans and cereal boxes well beyond their date of expiration. Amidst her tapes of classical music and videos of Broadway musicals were pornographic movies, presumably belonging to Tom.

Suddenly, I came across a handwritten note on lined paper from my mother to Anne—the words faded after forty years.

Dear Doinka,

"We've left the hospital and we're heading for home while Diane still feels okay. She's eager to 'get out of here.' Thanks for everything. It's all a memory now."

Love, Helen

Doinka, also spelled Dorogaya, was a Russian term of affection meaning "darling" that Anne and my mother occasionally used as sisters in tender moments. The note was dated May 17, 1960, the week after the surgery at Mercy Hospital in Cedar Rapids, a surgery that had liberated me from the catheter and marked the beginning of a newfound independence and freedom at age thirteen. Mother must have given the note personally to Anne since the envelope lacked postal information.

The chance of my finding this note after so many years was slim to none. First Anne would have to have saved it and then moved it with her from Iowa to Pennsylvania. Then I would have had to come here on impulse, move her out of her apartment, and stay to sort things before everything was thrown out. As I held that tangible insight into my past, I nodded to Jeff. "Our intuition was correct. We were meant to come here to help Anne, just as she had helped me."

As the work of starting my aunt on a new road to health and clearing out her old apartment progressed, I occasionally paused, reread the note and reflected on what it represented.

For my mother, the struggles of dealing with my health issues represented a memory best left behind, but for me, there was no leaving the past behind. Those memories of growing up with spina bifida, tethered to my father, troubled me in ways I was only beginning to understand.

When I was a child, being catheterized at home was normal for me, although it presented difficulties away from home. Not having anyone to talk with about this, I befriended someone I knew would understand—the big brother-looking Jesus. I saw his appearance every Sunday in church and on the prayer cards I received at Holy Communion at age seven. My communication with Jesus was silent. I didn't need words and didn't know how to put my concerns into words in any event. I didn't hear his voice. But knowing I could always imagine him close by provided steady reassurance.

On winter evenings, after Dad had layered on our beds the heavy patchwork quilts Grandma made, he left the room, I whispered to my childhood friend Jesus that he could come in now. Pulling back the covers, I made room for him and slept peacefully in his arms.

I prayed to his mother Mary using the rosary during the 10 to 15 minutes four times a day when Dad catheterized me.

I stretched out on the bed and pulled my pants down.

"Hail Mary, full of grace. The Lord is with thee. Blessed art thou among women, and blessed is the fruit of thy womb, Jesus."

Dad arrived with the catheter and pan.

"Holy Mary, Mother of God, pray for us sinners now and at the hour of our death. Amen."

"What are you doing?" Dad asked.

"I'm praying the Rosary," I said, holding up the white beads.

He inserted the catheter.

The First Joyful Mystery: The Annunciation: The Archangel Gabriel announces to Mary that she shall conceive the Son of God.

"Will you pray for me?" Dad asked.

Why should I pray for him? I wondered. I said nothing. Through my prayers, I hoped that I could take care of myself, that my bladder would start to work, that I could play like other kids, go to slumber parties and travel on field trips. Maybe I prayed as a way to focus on anything other than what was happening to me at that moment.

Yet, I sensed Dad *did* need prayer. We were both trapped in a routine, a procedure, neither of us had chosen. He faithfully tended to my needs and I acquiesced. No doubt both of us wished it could have been otherwise.

Friends continued to invite me to slumber parties and other events, many of which I declined because they would take me away from my parents for longer than my bladder would tolerate. Not confident in confronting my parents directly with this issue, I raised it indirectly. With friends Diane and Janice standing nearby, I begged to be able to go to their slumber party.

"Please let me go. It's just for an overnight," I said to them, knowing there was no way for this to work. Who would catheterize me?

"Not tonight, Diane. Maybe some other time," Dad brushed off my plea.

"But why not?" I persisted, knowing full well why not.

I wanted my friends to believe my strict parents kept me from joining them. But beyond that, I wanted to pressure my parents. What had been

OK was no longer OK. What they considered normal in my care was not normal at all. Something had to change.

"Your friends can come and stay overnight here," Dad said, a compromise that resolved the current situation but hardly addressed the underlying issue.

My emerging sexuality presented an even more difficult challenge. My parents were either deeply embarrassed or simply baffled about how to talk with me about the changes my body was undergoing. That's the only way I can make sense of what remains, even today, a troubling event in my past.

"We're going to Strawberry Point," Dad said. "Susie needs to see the doctor."

Why I needed to go along was unclear but perhaps Mother and Dad didn't want to leave me behind. We all climbed in the car and headed to Strawberry Point, a town of about 1000 people, large enough to support a family doctor and his practice. I didn't think to ask what was wrong with Susie. This style of communication was typical for our family—terse, especially when the matter at hand was delicate.

When we pulled up in front of the doctor's office, Dad turned around and said, "It's not Susie, it's you who needs to see the doctor."

Stunned, I followed them into the office while Susie waited behind in the car. With little explanation the nurse whisked us into the examining room, asked me to remove my shorts and panties and get up on the examining table. The doctor came in shortly, and without any comment, inserted a tube into my vagina and pushed something in. Careful orchestration of this sequence of events in advance meant no one had to explain anything.

At age 12, I didn't know the word "vagina," yet I knew something had been stuck inside me. I must have had some vaginal yeast infection, brought on by the continuous doses of sulfa I took every day to ward off urinary infections. This action was designed to treat it, but no one told me anything.

When he was through, I dropped off the table, pulled on my underwear, and stormed out of the office. Back in the car, I erupted. "Don't ever do that to me again!" And then with a catch in my throat, "Ever!"

I froze in my seat, my back pressed against the car seat, trying to get as far away from them as I could.

Neither Dad or Mother turned around to look at me nor did they say anything. Without ceremony, Dad drove us home.

My parents were decent people. I don't question whether they loved me. But the fact they approached this situation without realizing the emotional consequences for me tells me how unprepared they were to deal with my particular concerns and needs. They appeared to have no help in parenting, nor, as far as I know, did they seek it. Was such help even available at that time? I don't know. But from that point on, instinctively I began to look for help elsewhere.

As adolescents are wont to do, I discovered how good it felt to touch myself. Lacking any notion of privacy, since it had been taken from me long ago, I occasionally carried on this exploration as Dad prepared to catheterize me.

"Don't do that, Diane," he said, clearly horrified as he came into the room with the catheter in hand.

I stopped, immediately ashamed but also confused. He touched my genital area to insert a catheter, but I couldn't? Was it the timing, purpose, or the setting that mattered?

If that incident didn't signal that I was no longer a child, the official onset of puberty did.

It started routinely enough. I was now thirteen years of age. After dinner, I went as I always did into my parents' bedroom to be catheterized. Stretched out on the bed with my bottom near the edge, legs spread, I waited for Dad to arrive. He took off my diaper. His face whitened. He staggered back. His mouth fell open. He left without explanation. I peered down to see what he had reacted to. I gasped. Blood filled my diaper.

Mother came in a few moments later to explain about menstruation. "Diane, your period has started," she said gently. "There's nothing wrong. This is about the age it happens."

Girls typically started menstruating at age thirteen in that era. I had shown no signs of any difficulty. No cramps or stomachache. Nothing to indicate that life was about to change significantly for me.

For someone estranged from her body, as I was, this event profoundly shook me. Something beyond my control led to blood oozing from my genital area. Blood that came out of its own will and with its own timing. Finally, curiosity trumped horror.

"What happens now?" I asked Mother. My mother's hands shook, but she smiled reassuringly.

"Let's take care of you first," she said, using our euphemism for catheterizing.

She completed what Dad had started, by inserting the catheter and draining the urine. Then she explained about the pad I would wear to absorb the blood.

"So now I wear both a diaper and a pad?"

She nodded, her anguished face acknowledging the difficulty of an adolescent girl who must deal with both menstruation and incontinence.

At that moment I was no longer Daddy's little girl; I was too old to be dependent on him. Now, my mother would guide me in how to care for myself, or so I hoped. Mother turned to Anne for help. I can only imagine their conversation.

"Anne, this is Helen," my mother said. "We've talked before about Diane."

"Yes," Anne interrupted, "something needs to change."

"She started her period today."

"Helen, first of all, John must stop catheterizing Diane. This has gone on way too long."

"I know, but what are we going to do?"

"Let me talk to my friend who works for Dr. Parke, a urologist here in Cedar Rapids. Let's find out what he thinks we could do to help Diane go to the bathroom by herself."

"And what do I do in the meantime?"

"Helen, take care of Diane yourself. This is long overdue."

"Yes. (Sigh) I know."

So went a typical conversation between an older, more confident and dominant sister and a younger sister who frequently withdrew from uncomfortable situations and deferred to others. Yet, Mother reached out for help, and that's the memory of her I hold today.

Within a week, Mother and Dad talked to me about a surgery that a urologist in Cedar Rapids could do to help me empty my bladder. He most likely did a bladder neck incision and resection, a surgery done when other treatment options, such as drugs, did not solve the problem.

"You'll be in the hospital for a week until the doctor knows whether this works. I'll stay with Anne and Grandma and Grandpa," Mother explained.

"How long will it take? Will it hurt?" I asked.

"You'll be asleep the whole time, Honey, and we will be there when you wake up," she tried to assure me.

Amazed at how quickly my life was changing, I only nodded and prayed that this would work. The surgery scared me but also excited me. The risk was worth it if it meant I could be independent. Still I wondered, if the bladder neck opened more easily, would the bladder also leak more easily?

Soon we were on our way to Cedar Rapids to stay with Grandma and Grandpa and Anne in the early 1900s house they shared near the core of the city. We visited them often there—an inviting bungalow with a soft-cushioned sofa in the living room, oak wood trim, staircase and built-ins and a cozy kitchen where we often ate Kolaches from the Czech Village in the city. Early spring flowers already graced Grandma's large horseshoe-shaped garden in the backyard, inviting hummingbirds, cardinals, goldfinch and an array of other birds and insects to settle into their spring and summer home.

Susie and I shared an upstairs bedroom that night, a source of great comfort to me. She knew only that her sister was going to the hospital to have something done to her bladder. Later that night, as I tried to go to sleep, I heard her in a frightened voice pray the prayer to St. Jude for me, including the request to "come to my assistance in this hour of great need."

My sister and I, only 15 months apart in age, shared nearly everything growing up—our bedroom, our toys, our friends. A teacher once commented that as she watched the two of us walk home from school each day, she could tell we were not only sisters, but also friends. Now, we were sharing the anxiety of my surgery.

The next day my parents and I saw Dr. Parke at his office and then checked into the hospital. His examination the next morning was brief. Using a scope, he peered into the bladder and felt for its size and the contour of the bladder neck. An idea for the surgery, common at the time, had come to him as a possible solution. He assured us the chances of the surgery's working were encouraging.

The check-in and examination by the hospital staff exposed me to a larger world.

"What's this?" one of the nurses asked when she saw the diaper my mother made.

Lying on the examining table, surrounded by unfamiliar faces and unable to admit I wore a diaper, I turned my face to the wall, speechless.

"Maybe it's for her period," the nurse said to one of the technicians when it was clear I couldn't or wouldn't talk.

Up until then, my parents and I had managed to shield everyone outside the family from what happened to me daily. But now, in the glare of hospital examining rooms, this complete dependence on them and my childlike acquiescence, even at the age of thirteen, deeply embarrassed me.

The next morning at 5:00, people began to come into the room. The doctor who would give me the anesthesia explained that he would place a mask over my nose, and I would soon be asleep. A nurse checked my blood pressure, temperature and catheterized me.

Dad and Mother said they would be waiting for me after everything was over. Dr. Parke stopped in, this time in his operating room gown and hat, patted my hand and assured me everything was going to be fine.

Just what fine meant was still a mystery, but by then I was ready to find out.

My sense of time disappeared. Waking up hours later, I looked around the room. Mother and Dad were there. Mother jumped up when she saw me stir and came to the side of the bed and touched my arm.

"Diane, everything went well, just as Dr. Parke planned," she said.

Dad paced the perimeter of the room, looked out the window and then left briefly to smoke in the lounge. When he returned, I asked the question we all had been quietly thinking.

"Does this mean I can go to the bathroom by myself?"

"We need to wait to find out," they said, simultaneously repeating what the doctor had told them.

Within hours, my bladder was painfully full.

"Do you think you can get out of bed and go by yourself?" the nurse asked.

I began to cry.

I tried to sit up and drop my legs over the edge of the bed, but it hurt too much."

"I don't know. I don't know what to do. I need to go right now."

I fell back into the bed. I had failed. What should I be doing?

"You need to try," she responded.

"I can't try. Please help me."

Tears flooded my eyes. The nurse looked at me with mild disapproval. Why was I acting like a child? Did I expect to be catheterized even now—a young lady of 13?

She called Dr. Parke to find out what to do next. He instructed her to catheterize me. There was no time for delay. The stitches might come out if the bladder was stretched too much.

After that was done, I relaxed a bit but soon the pain intensified.

"I feel like crying," I said to my Dad, tears welling in my eyes.

"It's okay to cry," he responded.

"No, it hurts too much to cry," I sobbed.

"Don't cry, Diane. Would you do that for Daddy? Don't cry."

His request calmed me. I could do this for my

dad. Then I saw Mother crying as she stood behind him. Someone summoned the nurse and before long she came in the room with a needle filled with pain medicine.

The day after the surgery, the big test came. I went into the bathroom unaware of what I was to do except find some way to go. I sat on the stool and waited for something to happen. The urine was inside my bladder and I had to get it out. No message from my brain would release it, despite my attempts to communicate in this way.

So I pressed down hard on the lower abdomen, hoping to force it out. I didn't know if this was the way it worked and I didn't care. Success in peeing was my opportunity for independence. A spurt of urine escaped.

"I can go," I announced to the nurse. This was a triumph, I thought, yet also it raised an angry question. All this time, could I have pushed the urine out by myself? I'll never know. Despite my low-key announcement, a cheer went up in the nurses' lounge, I was told. The staff was rooting for me.

Now I just wanted to go home. Please, no more discussion, no more examinations, no more catheterization. This surgery, necessary or not, freed me from dependence on my parents. That was good enough for me, at least for now.

What happened that day should have happened years earlier. Today, children with spina bifida as young as five are taught to empty their bladders using a catheter, freeing them up to go to school and function somewhat normally.

My pressing down on the lower abdomen to push out the urine (later I learned this was the credé method) worked imperfectly, but it worked well enough to cut the cord that tethered me to my parents. I wanted to be a normal junior high girl, spending time with my friends without going home at regular intervals for help going to the bathroom.

Years later, when I traveled to State College to visit Aunt Anne, well before her relationship with Tom had begun, she told me that some things were "very good and others were very bad" about my childhood.

Characteristically I didn't ask what she meant, but now I can fill in the blanks. Very good was the love I experienced in my home. "Very bad" was my Dad's well-meaning but intrusive involvement with my body.

"That wasn't very helpful," my art therapist said later when I reported this conversation. "Didn't she say anything else?"

No, she didn't. Neither did she ever blame anyone for anything. Nor do I. My parents did everything they knew how to do. While they likely held on too long to their fear and concern about me, they shepherded me through my childhood and adolescent years, and I am alive today. Whatever resentment or anger I once had, I have long ago released.

Anne's identification of a surgeon to close my spine when I was an infant happened she said, "only because I happened to be sitting in the cafeteria at the University of Iowa and started talking to this neurosurgeon."

But I now know how active she was behind the scenes finding a way to rescue me—and rescue all of us. Dad needed help releasing his obsessive-compulsive concern about keeping me infection free and his belief that only he could ensure this. Mother needed help asserting herself and finding a way to free both her and me from Dad's controlling behavior. I needed help going to the bathroom by myself and, more fundamentally, beginning a life of my own.

Aunt Anne accepted her new living situation with dignity, although she continued to ask about Tom. Her letters to me during this time in the nursing home speak of the thrill she experienced in watching a favorite musical on television, her appreciation for copies of CDs and DVDs friends and family made for her, and a favorite Bible verse (Mathew 25:40—*Truly I tell you, just as you did it to one of the least of these who are members of my family, you did it to me*).

Our family needed an Aunt Anne—someone

who broke the silence, spoke the truth and acted with boldness, even as she sometimes caused
consternation, disrupted family routines, and
alarmed us with her eccentric, even bizarre, behavior. She needed us too in the end.

RESILIENCE CHOREOGRAPHED?

Once you have survived both spina bifida and breast cancer, once you have lived through failed relationships and left a marriage, once you have given up a career and begun rediscovering what you really want, and when people remark over and over again about your resilience, you do start to wonder. Is what you thought of as simply putting one foot in front of another, of changing direction as needed, of learning new steps when the old ones lost relevance or effectiveness, of surrendering to the lead of others and accepting your dependence—is this *resilience?* Or merely acquiescence to what confronted you, over and over again?

I had done all of these things and *still* loved my life. I was blessed with Jeff, a tender, sweet man and my husband, someone given to telling me frequently how much I enlivened his life and how dear I was to him. I had meaningful work as a spiritual director. Although health issues still loomed on the horizon, I knew that, in the past, I had gamely worked through them as they arose.

A "sisters' trip" Eileen, Susie and I had decided to take to revisit our old childhood home in Arlington provided an opportunity to mull over these thoughts and search for the source of my resilience, if that indeed was what it was. In touring our house, would I recall inspiring memories of enjoying life despite the recurring challenges? Or would such a visit drag up things better forgotten, myself as a reluctant participant in life, or worse, a victim? Would it help me to understand how this childhood, and specifically my family, had shaped the adult I had become?

I wondered, "Was the front yard always this small?" as Eileen, Sue and I pulled up to our house. More than 40 years had passed since we had stepped inside this small, white bungalow on Main Street in a rural Iowa farming community of 429 people.

We had talked about our lives for hours as we traveled from Des Moines, leaving behind Jeff, Eileen's husband Larry and Susie's husband Fausto for their own guys' retreat, grilling steaks on the deck of our home and relaxing in the mild summer weather.

"The bushes in front of the house are gone," Susie said as we sat in the car, staring at a yard, both familiar and strange.

"The house looks plain and small without them," I added. The bushes, actually tall cedars, had edged either side of the front porch and gave the exterior of the house symmetry and a degree of class that the now ordinary-looking house no longer had.

"The shed next door and the goat that lived there have disappeared," Eileen noted.

"And do you remember the horse that was tied up in the neighbor's back yard?" Susie asked. "It was thin and not well cared for. Mother objected to what she saw as its cruel treatment. She and Dad went to the city council to have it removed." The recollection brought back all the ways Mother identified with animals—the birds she tended at feeders, the poems she wrote about "God's creatures," and the continuing stream of pets she and Dad welcomed into our home.

Mrs. Shumway's giant cottonwood trees across the street still towered like stately dowagers, although she had long since passed away, and her house was gone, leaving an empty lot. On stormy days, I sat on the front porch and watched those trees sway, trying to guess whether they would reach our house if they fell. On snowy days, Mrs. Shumway paid us a nickel to retrieve her letters and bills from a difficult-to-reach mailbox.

We assessed the house—no obvious paint

peeling or sagging roof-line. I eyed the steps of the front porch with curiosity. Susie and I sat on those steps every day in the late afternoon, weather permitting, waiting for Dad to return home. They looked solid, a sturdy welcome into the home.

"That's one of my favorite memories," Dad frequently said. "You girls sitting on the porch, waiting for me."

How would it feel now to sit on that porch with Susie? I wondered. I decided to save this part of the tour—sitting on that porch with Susie—until the end of our visit.

"Come on in," Abby, the blonde young, friendly schoolteacher who owned our old house, said as she responded to our knock on the front door. "Are you Eileen?" she said to my older sister who had arranged our visit. She waved her hand into the living room and stepped aside so we could enter.

"Take your time and go wherever you want," she said, graciously giving us permission to wander without her.

Entering the living room, I scanned the four walls encompassing the ten-by-twelve-foot space. In my memory, I saw the television we acquired in 1953, housed in a dark wood console along with a radio, resting in front of the windows framed by the flowered drapes Mother made. Like most of America at that time, we drank in hours of "I Love Lucy," "Gunsmoke," "The Hit Parade" and other shows popular in the 50s and 60s. Every night I stayed up until l0 p.m. to watch an airplane soar across the TV screen to the sound of the Star Spangled Banner, a signal that programming would then stop. My spirit soared with that plane, if only for seconds, as I imagined life beyond our little home.

My eyes moved to the wall where our beloved piano once stood, a Kimball upright that Mother bought at an estate sale for $50 soon after she and Dad married. Made of dark wood with warm cherry undertones, showing a few nicks and scratches and featuring real ivory keys that were barely yellow and fully intact, the piano sounded a bright clear tone, one that had satisfied me through years of piano lessons during elementary and junior high.

"Diane, are you ready to take the piano with you?" Mother asked soon after my first marriage. It was as if that was always the piano's destiny—to grace my home, much as it had my mother's. It moved seven times from my first apartment as a newlywed to a century farmhouse I shared with Jeff. It served me well when I studied piano lessons as an adult at Drake University in Des Moines.

This piano was the one on which I played Edvard Grieg's melodies brought together in the musical, *Song of Norway*. Romantic and emotional as a child, I swelled with the anguish and rapture of the music, stroking the keys with exaggerated feeling. It was the piano on which I memorized "Claire de Lune" and played "Pavanne to a Dead Princess" over and over again, trying the patience of my family who might have preferred a more diverse or upbeat repertoire.

That Pavanne became a theme song of my practicing as I sought with my pre-teen sensibilities to recreate the bittersweet feelings of the piece. Far from being a dead princess, I nonetheless felt a sense of loss I could not yet name.

"Does anyone like this song?" I called out to a silent and until then unresponsive house, seeking affirmation after playing dozens of renditions.

"I like it, Diane!" Dad responded from the other room. It was all the encouragement I needed to play it again.

My favorite times, however, occurred when Mother and I played duets, snuggling close together on the piano bench with its padded top and ornate side panels, another find she purchased at a house sale. The top was broken in two, but the exotic beauty of the side carvings more than compensated for its split seat.

"If you ever recover this bench, Diane," she advised, "remember that the top was in two pieces." Mother had a gift for taking things someone else might have thrown out and making them beautiful. Even then it was assumed I would be the beneficiary of not only the piano but also Mother's love for classical music. The recovered bench now sits in the bar of our condo, surrounded by covers of ragtime piano music written by women.

She and I made contests of our duet playing, racing to finish first. Grieg's "Anitra Tanz" or Dance of Anitra particularly suited this competition. In both the Secondo and the Primo parts, Anitra sprinted across the keys with staccato frenzy, as we hastened with speed toward the end.

Mother's delighted laugh would end the piece regardless of who finished first. I was the better sight-reader of music but she played by ear, which I could not. Beyond that, during these times she seemed happy. Regardless of life circumstances, she found a *way* to be happy, using music to enhance or sometimes transcend what was happening around her. I smiled, remembering those moments.

Resting for a moment on the couch, I felt other memories surface. In summer months, I often read a book a day in this room, devouring the adolescent literature of the day. Like a lot of young girls, I loved Nancy Drew—her exploits, her courage, her dismissal of convention, her persistence in meeting challenges and finding unlikely solutions, sometimes with others and sometimes, if necessary, all by herself. When I exhausted the young people's section, I dove into adult literature, raising the eyebrows of the town librarian.

"Does your Mother know you're reading this?" she once asked.

"Yes, of course," I responded quickly, putting

the latest adult fiction book on the bottom of my stack of textbooks. Mother didn't know, but neither did she closely check what I was reading and I never knew if she would have cared.

I had started "Marjorie Morningstar" by Herman Wouk. Marjorie begins her young life idealistic and determined to pursue her dreams but ends up living a life that resembles her parents' more limited existence. When I reached the part of the story where Marjorie "bares her breasts," in the words of the novel, to an older man, I stopped reading. At age 12, I wasn't quite ready to learn about premarital sex. And maybe I didn't want to know about a woman who settles for a life smaller than the one she wanted.

Setting those recollections aside, I moved into the dining room, lit by a double window facing the back yard of the house. When we lived there, wide-paneled Venetian blinds covered the windows. My only regular household chore, aside from making my bed and helping with the supper dishes, was dusting those blinds every week, a responsibility Mother assigned to Susie and me. We did it willingly, only occasionally needing a prompt.

Under the dining room table, Susie and I created a house to play in, covering the table with a blanket and converting the space in between each of the ornate pedestal legs into separate rooms. We brought our Ginny dolls to this imaginary mansion, as well as their Ginny doll wardrobes and all the clothes—evening gowns, furry wraps, dresses and sweaters—that Mother made for them.

She also created beds for them, wielding a saw and paint brush with amazing confidence. The construction took place in the basement of the house, an unfinished space of cement walls dripping with humidity, of lone bulbs providing dim pools of light, and of numerous centipedes, spiders, and other insects. Susie and I ventured down there only when our play called for ghoulish settings or complete secrecy—or in this case because Mother was engaged in something especially for us.

"Mommy, what are you doing?" Susie asked.

"Your dolls need beds," she said.

"They do?" Susie asked wide-eyed.

"Of course, silly," I interjected. "Our dolls need to sleep just like we do!"

As we chattered away, Mother set up her work station—an old wooden table that came with the house, her hand-held saw with its wooden handle, and large pieces of plywood Dad brought home for her. We watched as she sawed the large boards into three smaller pieces for each bed—a platform six inches by ten and two end pieces for the foot and head.

After she had nailed the three parts together, she sanded and smoothed the edges and then painted the beds white. In retrospect, I realize the beds were plain but in our eyes they were wondrous works, perfect for their little inhabitants. Like us, our dolls would feel safe and comfortable. Mother could make anything!

The 8-inch Ginny doll introduced in 1951 had become a fixture in many American homes by 1957. Susie and I were desperate to have one.

"Daddy, there's a toy store down the street," Susie piped up. We were eating at a restaurant for Sunday dinner.

"It's not likely to be open, Susie," Dad remarked, returning to the business of eating. "Stores are closed on Sundays."

"But can't we look?" she persisted.

Her questioning prompted a walk to the store after dinner was over. Remarkably, it was open.

Susie and I scanned the dolls in the window, spotting the diminutive Ginny dolls with various hair colors and styles in dresses, play clothes, and pajamas. We gazed into their sweetly drawn faces, pressing our noses and foreheads into the glass. Mother, equally charmed, announced we must go inside to look.

"Those dolls are perfect for the girls," she told Dad as she opened the door and entered the store.

I suspect Dad could see the decision had already been made, but he granted the permission anyway by saying, "You can each pick out a doll and one other thing." Susie opted for a little Ginny Doll hat and I selected a suitcase, anticipating my doll would travel.

I glanced around the dining room again and in my mind's eye could see the console record turntable and radio and Mother's 33 1/3 LPs. At Mother's initiative, we listened to Rachmaninoff, Tchaikovsky, Grieg, and Broadway musicals like *The King and I*, *Brigadoon*, *Finian's Rainbow*, and *Music Man*.

Later, Eileen, turning into a teenager, crooned over The Platters. We made fun of her fascination with not only The Platters but also with Elvis. At that age, we were too young to respond to Elvis' gyrations, yet when the Beatles came along in 1964, we squealed along with every other high school girl in the country.

On the far right wall was a breakfront housing Mother's prized possessions—a blue Wedgwood vase and the good China, an ivory Lenox plate with a cranberry band and gold rim. But the most prized possession of all was a pearly white marble birdbath with birds poised along the edges. What was it about that birdbath that charmed her so? Knowing how much Mother loved it, Eileen, Sue and I now share it, rotating it from one home to another since she died. It now resides with me and has for several years.

Our parents' bedroom fronted the house, parallel to the living room. Although Abby had decorated it smartly, and it was well lit, in my memory the room was dim with shades drawn. An old wooden double bed, stained pink, took up most of the room, together with a matching dresser.

Staring at the place where that bed stood, I shivered, remembering Dad bringing in the hot washcloth and towels, white lacquer pan, and the sterilized catheter from the kitchen, morning, noon and night, requiring me to scoot to the edge of the bed, open my legs and wait for him to insert the rubber tube.

Our parents' bedroom also brought up memories of Mother's hours of daytime sleeping. She spent a good deal of her afternoon curled up on top of that bed, a blanket covering her quiet, seemingly immovable frame. During that time, we instinctively knew the house must be quiet — no music, no laughter, as little chatter as possible. In the summer months that usually meant we played outside, often badminton, riding our bikes or visiting friends.

At 3:30 p.m. every day Susie and I walked to the Cottage Inn a block away on Main Street to buy Mother a piece of pie. She preferred peach if the fruit was in season, or apple, if it was not. Just not raisin, for sure, she always reminded us. A waitress placed it on a paper plate, covered it with foil and we carried it home.

Susie pulled me from my thoughts. "Look, Diane, they haven't fixed the doorknob on this bedroom door!"

She was in the small bedroom adjacent to the bath that first served as Eileen's room and then became Susie's. Susie and my cousin Kathy were playing in the room's closet once when I, just to be mean, leaned against the door and locked it, forgetting that, without a doorknob, it could not be opened. Terrified they might suffocate and feeling guilty I had caused this problem, I blew air into the closet through a straw, hoping my sister and cousin would not run short of oxygen. Then I alerted Mother, who was forced to dash uptown to the smoke-filled tavern where Dad often played poker in the evenings, find him and summon him to come home and take off the door. The whole incident amused Susie and Kathy, but I felt both bad and responsible because I knew it deeply embarrassed my mother, who had to enter a province reserved in our small town for men.

I moved to the stairs, leading to the attic, a magical retreat for me during junior and senior high schools. At the top of those stairs, Mother put her sewing machine, and there she escaped to dream up and make her beautiful creations. I followed her example, making most of my clothes—dresses, skirts and blouses that I could hardly have afforded if we had traveled to Waterloo to buy them. I eyed the space now, noting that the battered linoleum floor had not changed in those four decades. My memories of sewing were equally unchanged.

After placing the patterns on fabric stretched out on the dining room table and pinning them down, I cut out each piece. Then, I took the pieces, which were to be joined, up those stairs, pinned them together and eased them under the needle, making sure I backstitched at the beginning and end of each seam. Sleeve tops were more difficult than straight seams. I had to loosely hand stitch each one so they could be gathered slightly and fit into the bodice. Then I would double stitch around the top of the skirt, gather it evenly, and fit it into the waistband I had already made. Buttonholes, carefully made with a special attachment, anchored the blouses and jackets. By following the instructions inside the pattern envelope and knowing my own body, I became skilled at making everything fit.

I remembered going to fabric stores, inhaling the fragrance of bolts of material, stroking the varying surfaces as I walked up and down the aisles, luxuriating in the color, and reading pattern books as if they were novels. There I could imagine something whole and beautiful. There I knew that if I had a vision, I had the means to accomplish it. There, I suspect, the embryonic idea took shape in me that the unusual pieces of my life could be fit together into something wonderful.

Sitting at that sewing machine spot at the top of the stairs helped me rise above the tribulations of my leaky bladder and bouts of leg pain that started during a growth spurt when I was seven or eight years old. There I could control my own reality. While hearing the hubbub below me and appreciating the family it represented, there

I could escape, at least for a time, the limitations imposed on my life. The old Singer machine with its floor pedals whirred in a way that comforted me as little else did in those days. Only the heat of the mid-summer day in a house lacking air conditioning could drive me away.

Coming back down the stairs, I wandered into the kitchen, the smallest room in the house aside from the bathroom. Painted a soft aqua, Mother's favorite color, it had barely four feet of counter space, a single sink, and a small ceramic table with a yellow and black pattern that my friend Becky called the "bumblebee table." It was just large enough for the four of us to crowd around while Mother or Dad served us. Once Eileen became a teenager, she was rarely home for supper, preferring the company of her friends.

In the mornings, the aroma of the bacon Dad cooked in preparing us for school wafted from the kitchen. Getting us off to school was his responsibility. That meant not only feeding us, but also checking our clothes, holding our chins steady in one hand as he brushed our hair with the other, and catheterizing me. He never showed impatience or lost his temper in doing so, although we sometimes gave him reason to do just that. Why wasn't Mother there helping? We never even wondered, assuming, I suppose, that she needed her sleep.

Day after day. Year after year. The routine was the same. But one day was different. After Dad had fried my eggs, slid them onto a plate, and placed the plate on the table in front of me, I felt something in me breaking. This time I couldn't hold it together. Instead of picking up my fork, I picked up my plate, turned away from the table and hurled it at the wall. A loud cracking noise broke the silence as the plate landed and easy-over eggs splatted and then slid down the aqua paint.

I pushed back tears that were flooding my eyes and averted my father's quick glance, suddenly feeling ashamed for ruining the breakfast he had made for me, for breaking our well-established routine, for—I didn't know—perhaps for wanting something different.

Surprised by this unexpected outburst, my father, quickly said, "That's okay, honey," as he wiped the mess off the wall. "We all have bad days."

It's hard to imagine that other parents would not have asked their child something like, "Why did you do that?" Or, "What's going on?" Or at least required her to help clean up. He was either being incredibly kind or he was afraid to ask me what was wrong. Perhaps, he didn't want to know about problems he couldn't solve or things he couldn't fix. My problem, whatever it was, was not fixable. So, like most conversations in our family, this one never took off. Without words to express what was most likely anger, an emotion rarely if ever displayed in our household, I spoke in the only way available at that moment.

With a children's edition of a Better Home and Garden cookbook, which we'd been given, Susie and I would look for a reason to make our favorite recipes, especially the sugar cookies with maraschino cherries and white frosting.

"Diane, do you feel like sugar cookies?" Susie would ask. That's all it took, and we were busily emptying cups of flour and sugar from the coun-tertop metal canisters into bowls.

"Here, you cream the butter and sugar," I di-rected Susie while I sifted together the flour, salt, baking powder and soda.

"Do you think Mother will mind?" Susie asked.

"No, everyone will eat them for supper along with the soup," I reasoned.

Supper, what we called the evening meal, was light—typically a can of Campbell's chicken noo-dle soup, divided four ways, and a lunch-meat sandwich on white bread.

Having made the cookies many times, we worked quickly. The cookie sheets came out. We pulled out a jar of maraschino cherries from the refrigerator, lit the oven, and began combin-ing ingredients. Before long, the entire house smelled of cookies. We sampled each batch. Yes, they were all excellent. Perfectly baked cookies would be only slightly brown on the bottom when we took them from the oven since they cooked a minute or two more before being removed from the sheet.

Later as I studied Home Economics in junior high, I attempted to duplicate at home with some success the pies we made in class. However, I ignored other cooking lessons like how to clean and bake chickens and can tomatoes. Although we lived in farm country, I didn't see myself as the farm wife my teacher envisioned and chose to stick to the sweeter side of life. Not every experiment in the kitchen produced pleasing fragrances. After Christmas one year, having been given a chemistry set by Mother and Dad, I started cooking concoctions that smelled up the entire house and occasionally caught fire.

In the afternoon in summer, Susie and I converted the kitchen into a grocery store, hauling out all the canned and packaged goods inside the cupboards and "selling" them to one another. As long as we were quiet in our pursuits, no one minded. In our small house in this little town, I felt independent and free to do what I wanted to do.

Eileen rejoined our home tour and, as a group, we sisters moved out the back door to the patio, a concrete slab just outside the kitchen door.

"Remember when we would set those old bucket and butterfly chairs out here and sit and watch the cars go by?" Susie laughed.

"Do you know who that is?" we said in unison, laughing, mimicking the question we always asked as a car went by.

I claimed the patio as my unofficial office in the summer. There I set up my three-by-three-foot child's play table. In an act that asserted there was indeed a world outside our household, I began my study of the country and the world. Writing to each state capital in the U.S., I asked for information about their state, places to go, and things to do. Though barely 10 years old, I obviously impressed people enough to be put on their mailing lists. Soon catalogs, maps, and brochures began to arrive in large manila envelopes.

"Is there anything for me?" I'd ask when the mail arrived, but more often than not, I was the one to retrieve letters from the front porch and sort them by addressee. Almost daily, one state or another sent promotional material, often in the form of large envelopes with out-of-state return addresses.

"It's Virginia today," I shouted out, checking off another state on my list. This particular mailing was a bonanza—a state map, a colorful 30-something-page booklet filled with pictures of tourist sites, a paperback history of Virginia, and a letter from the Governor.

I giggled at the message in his letter. "Come to Virginia," he said, inviting me to stop into the state capitol for a look-around. "Visit as a tourist but stay as a resident," he continued. I could move there, start a business or find a job in their growing industries.

I created files for each state, placed the files in cardboard boxes that rested on the concrete and waited for who knows what. The term "travel agent" may not have existed in the 1950s. Yet, I was on my way to being equipped to provide information on sightseeing activities in every area of the country or advising would-be entrepreneurs on business opportunities.

My interest also extended outside the continental U.S., as I clipped maps of countries around the world from the newspaper and magazines. My interest at this point was primarily visual. I loved examining the contours of each country, its land features, rivers, mountains and where the major cities were located. I pasted the maps on heavy sheets of construction paper.

Standing there on the patio, remembering all my projects, I felt a rush of love for my mother, who had been too often absent from my memories. Yet it was Mother who encouraged my efforts by taking out her saw and making a scrapbook cover. Mother who helped me punch holes in each of the sheets. Mother who found shoelaces that we ran through the pages and cover to hold the book together. Mother who saved this scrapbook through moves from Iowa to Pennsylvania to Texas. Decades later, after she died, my sisters retrieved it from her belongings to give to me.

Before my sisters and I made this trip, we had reviewed old family photos. My favorite showed our entire family draped across the front steps of our house, looking happy and relaxed. A separate photo showed Mother and Dad together on the steps, Mother's full skirt fanning out gracefully and Dad's arm circling her. Those photos and this visit back to our family home reinforced for me how nearly normal my childhood was for that era in the rural Midwest.

Yes, I had to return home to my parents for help going to the bathroom. That was decidedly not normal. But that ritual didn't prevent my exploration of the world through books, through hobbies, through playtime with my sisters, through my music and through my academic endeavors. My curiosity eased me through difficulties that otherwise might have been overwhelming.

Mother and Dad didn't get everything right. Few parents do. But they succeeded in delivering as much normalcy as they could imagine and orchestrate. Before they died, Mother in 2003, and Dad nine years later, I had numerous opportunities to tell them how much I appreciated all they did for me as a child. And they told me over and over again how proud they were of me, how much I had accomplished, and "more or less on your own."

"You did this yourself, Diane," Mother said to me one day "You, of all of us, have really done something with your talents."

So, yes, I had shown resilience, but I learned it from the people around me and from life itself. It's a skill you acquire when others challenge you, when they show you the way, when they leave you alone, when they step in to rescue you from problems too big or complicated to solve by yourself. When they teach you through example that happiness is ultimately something only you can find for yourself.

The trip home fulfilled my expectations and more. Now, it was time to leave.

"Susie, let's sit on the front steps, just like we used to," I said. Eileen stayed behind, chatting with our house's owner, which gave us a chance to recreate our childhood memory. We went out the side door, across the concrete patio and to the front of the house.

Did I sit on the right or the left? Were we on the wooden porch or one of the steps? Did we talk or were we quiet as we looked for Dad? Neither of us could remember, so, leaving behind the chatter, we sat down. I moved close to Susie and wrapped my arm around her. At that moment, my world became as small as that porch. But as we rose to leave, it became, once again, as big as the worlds of my scrapbook. The gentle sound of birds and whirl of the wind sang to me as it had decades ago, assuring me that I belonged as the traveler, as the dancer, I had become.

"THIS NEED TO DANCE"

I cleared my throat, "Ladies, it's time to dance! Listen to the music. Let your bodies take the lead. Dance around the entire room. It's time to let go. No one will be watching you."

As I called these directions, women left their art projects, small group discussions and solitary reflection to rejoin others in the center of this cavernous room. Together with my friend and colleague Deb, I was leading a retreat at the Sinsinawa Monastery near Galena, Illinois, designed to help women discover and express their unique creativity and spirituality.

As sounds of Bonnie Raitt's "Love Letter" resonated throughout the room (we had turned the volume up as high as it would go), women began to swing their arms and move their feet. What they did beyond that I don't know. I quickly got lost in my own dancing.

Taken over by the music, yearning to move, desiring to be sensuous, and oblivious and indifferent to what others thought, I traveled the room with ease. Arms opening gracefully, shoulders rolling rhythmically, eyes searching alluringly, legs striding effortlessly, pelvis rotating naturally—that's what I imagine my dance looked like. I don't know for sure. All I know is how it felt from the inside.

For the few minutes of that song, I fully occupied every cell of my body. I reveled in its shape, its movement, its poise. There was nothing to be ashamed of, nothing to hide, nothing to protect. I had no apologies or explanations to offer. This body was healthy, whole, feminine, and beautiful. *I* was healthy, whole, feminine, and beautiful.

"I wish I could be that spontaneous and free," another woman who happened to have spina bifida said, perhaps fearing, like me, the possibility of her bladder leaking.

My bladder did leak a little, but I didn't care. It too had a right to dance with abandon and joy. The retreat ended, but the confidence I felt that day stayed with me. When someone or something invites me to dance either literally or figuratively, I dance. Moving to life's rhythms has become part of who I am.

My relationship with Jeff opened up a new expressiveness and confidence in my life. He loved my body, even with all its scars. If he came into the room when I happened to be naked, he always responded with playful enthusiasm.

"You're beautiful!" "Caught you!" "You look enticing."

During lovemaking, he kisses me both passionately and tenderly, stroking the scars on my chest where my breasts had been and the scars on my lower back and buttocks where the doctor had closed my spine. But it wasn't as if he made a special effort to do that; it was all part of taking in my whole body. Jeff's belief that I was beautiful, not to mention my emerging pride in and gratitude for this body that had survived so much, brought with it a new sense of ease and peace.

In contrast, throughout much of my childhood and early adulthood, I had fought to break out of some perceived barrier—an attitude or belief that life as an attractive woman who enjoyed her sexuality lay beyond my reach. I witnessed this barrier in a very dramatic and visual way one day in an image that emerged just as I was awakening from a nap.

In my early forties, a decade before my cancer diagnosis, Eileen, Susie and I vacationed together for the first time in years. We decided to stay on Maui at an Embassy Suites. A beautiful crystal blue pool shimmered like a jewel outside our window. On lazy mornings, we sat by the pool indulging in French toast, Mimosas and fruit from a luscious buffet. It was my first real opportunity to relax after months of flying around the country as a consultant to candidates for Congress and Governor.

Free time and a comfortable sofa enticed me into an after-lunch snooze. Slowly awakening after just a half hour or so, I saw it, or rather I saw *someone*. The stone wall of a cave, cold, hard, and dripping with moisture, loomed before me. What was this? A vision? A half-asleep dream?

Then I saw the eyes. Two eyes in the cave wall. Staring out without expression. They would have escaped my notice except they blinked. The angle of the eyes suggested they belonged to someone lying in the wall horizontal with the ground. Was this person trapped, imprisoned, and unable to move?

The eyes appeared sad. Was a tear escaping from one of them? At clock-like intervals, something was inserted in between what seemed like the legs of this person, machine-like, without emotion. Over and over again. She couldn't stop it. She couldn't change the timing. She could only lie very still.

Hearing Eileen and Sue talking and about ready to enter the room, I knew my time to respond was limited.

"I don't know how, but I will free you from that wall," I reassured this person who had by now become a young girl in my mind. "I'm not abandoning you. I'm putting you safe inside me where you'll be protected."

That was all I could do at the moment.

"Are you ready for lunch?" Eileen asked, reaching for her purse and glancing out the window. "What a gorgeous, sunny day!"

Gathering up my scattered thoughts and feelings, I pulled myself together, pretending nothing had happened. The image of that cave wall, those eyes, the resignation, and the sense of invasion and loneliness they conveyed, burned inside my mind and heart. I felt too heavy to move. My chest sank in an attempt to contain all this emotion within me. I would not forget the girl I was carrying.

Weeks later, the image still haunting my waking hours, I confided to my massage therapist about this dilemma, without attempting to interpret what it meant.

"I have this girl in a wall inside me. I need to free her," I stuttered. How strange and scary this image must have sounded.

Lying face up on the therapist's table, I told her a bit more. The cold, wet walls of the cave, the eyes that occasionally blinked letting me know the girl was still there, the dark, cool air.

"Can you go back and visually free her?" my therapist suggested as she continued the massage. "Perhaps you can bring sunlight into the space or plant a garden."

"Like an inner garden?" I responded, beginning to see the possibilities.

"Yes, find a quiet time and space to meditate and create the whole scene, entering the cave, seeing her there, speaking to her, doing whatever feels freeing and healing," she continued.

Over the next few months, I visited this girl in the wall. The sunlight traveled with me, filling up the previously dark space and warming up the cold wall. A gentle stream began to flow through, bringing soil to fill the crevices in the floor. Seeds became stems and leaves, later producing flowers. The walls softened. Cracks began to form. Eventually, the walls crumbled, and I was there to catch the little girl and hold her in my arms.

"It's okay. You're free. You can leave this space or come back if you need to, but we can go now," I told her. She nodded but said nothing. Years later, she would talk and share her story of how she came to claim and live in her body.

For a naïve, sexually inexperienced young woman from small-town Iowa, the move to Chicago in 1969 challenged what I believed to be true about the world and my place in it. Women could do whatever they were capable of doing. So I thought. Yet, in the publishing company where I worked, women could be secretaries and editorial assistants, but not salesmen. "The men you call on will be more interested in you than in the books you are selling," my boss explained when I approached him about moving into sales.

Unfortunately for me, I chose my first sexual experience in life with that same boss, a man 13 years my senior. Looking back on it now, I wonder how I could have been so foolish. But, he was attractive to me, I had never had sex, and I chose to pursue him—or did he pursue me?

"Diane, you're a nice girl," he said to me in the car as he was taking me home after a meeting. His hand reached over and lightly touched my knee, just a whisper of a touch that could have been an accident.

"I like you," I confessed. "You have such beautiful eyes." His eyes were an intense blue, and I shivered when they lingered on me longer than necessary. Was he inviting me into a relationship? He parked his Mercedes in front of the modest brick building near Lake Michigan where I had found an apartment affordable on my editorial assistant's salary.

"Can I come in?" Fear and excitement clutched me as I nodded yes.

"I'm a virgin," I admitted as we tousled in bed removing the last of our clothing. The strains of Rachmaninoff's "Variations on a Theme by Paganini," one my favorite Romantic pieces, soared from the stereo in the living room.

"Then this could hurt a little," he explained, "and perhaps you'll bleed."

Our nakedness shocked me. Moments before we were business associates in professional clothing. Now we were nude, completely vulnerable, completely available to one another's body. Did he like what he saw? Was my body desirable, even given the scars on my back? No one had seen my breasts before. Would they somehow make up for what I considered my body's flaws?

"You're beautiful, you know. Kind of like an Earth Mother," he said as he explored my body.

An Earth Mother? I didn't know what that meant, but it sounded normal, even lovable.

His hands stroked me gently yet persistently. He was not going to stop, and I didn't want him to stop.

"You're lovely down there, you know," he whispered in my ear.

Something hard pressed against my thigh and soon it was over. It hurt a little, and my bladder released. If he noticed, he didn't say anything. And I didn't explain.

After that one encounter, I knew what a big mistake I had made. How could we work together pretending this had not happened? I blamed myself for using him to give me this first experience, but I was also mortified to learn that he sexually pursued one of the other young editorial assistants in the office not long after our short-lived encounter. He was a powerful executive and my boss and I was a 22-year old virgin who had just moved from Iowa to the big city. And yet, I took full responsibility for the evening and all that happened afterward. Regardless of who was responsible, I learned an important lesson. When I act out physical desire without honesty and emotional commitment, the outcome is damaging.

Dancing, in this case folk dancing, helped me survive those lonely, confusing days in this big, strange city.

"Look," I whispered to the young woman sitting next to me at the publishing company where I worked, like me an editorial assistant. "The Folk Dance Club in this neighborhood near the lake is inviting me to join. Let's check it out!"

"I don't know how to folk dance," she responded warily.

"I don't know much. I took folk dance in college as a way to get out of taking tougher P.E. courses. I was no athlete. Come on. It will be fun. We'll learn."

She agreed. Before long, we spent our free evenings doing the Schottische, the Reel, the Polka, and Greek circle dances, stumbling at first to learn the steps and keep up with the experienced dancers, but eventually taking our place among this group of folk dance loyalists. We were the youngsters there, likely a welcome addition to an aging group concerned about expanding its ranks.

The leader of the group eyed me with respect as my legs hopped, stepped, swung, and pivoted in perfect rhythm to the sounds of the music. Perhaps I was channeling my Russian grandmother who danced in her home country of the Ukraine. Regardless of where my energy or skill came from, the exhilaration of these evenings erased for a time the disaster occurring at work.

Not surprisingly, the affair with my boss ended after that night, and the job ended a few months later. I left Chicago and moved to Iowa to take a job teaching high school English and journalism. And I began looking for a marriage partner. In the 1960s and 1970s, women expected to marry in their 20s. I was 24 when I took that job, and it was time to get married.

Through friends, I met a local man, whose shyness and reclusiveness somehow drew me in. He felt familiar—and I liked him. But more significantly, I thought I could help him. I would be the catalyst for him to connect and socialize with others. We would have friends, invite people over, go to concerts, and yes, we'd make love. He was a virgin, he said, and sexual activity was still new for me aside from my errant one-time relationship with my boss.

"Do you realize what we're doing?" he asked one day early in our marriage, incredulous that two adults could do these things without the police rushing in. It wasn't that our sex life was so exotic. I see now that we were simply two immature adults, brought together by our insecurities and inexperience. But something was missing. Some intimacy unrelated to sex.

"You're like a little flower," he said to me once,

in what was probably the most tender and memorable moment of our relationship.

But fundamental problems refused to be suppressed. I didn't love him like he deserved to be loved. He eventually acknowledged his agoraphobia. During our year of marriage counseling, we traveled to Des Moines once a week, which required him to fight his panic response, get in the car, and take deep breaths while I drove him to our appointment.

After several months of sessions, the therapist summed up what he saw.

"You two have so many secrets from one another. Yours is a relationship with little intimacy."

I noticed an ad in the paper for some new kind of marriage therapy, therapy that you could do as a couple or alone. It was sexual therapy, a weird concept in my mind, but not uncommon in the 1970s, and I decided I wanted to go—alone. It was stranger than even I had imagined.

"Close your eyes and take several deep breaths. Imagine your breath coming in and out of your genital area," the workshop leader instructed, as we lay on the floor of the church sanctuary.

What a curious idea, I thought, but I was game for almost anything. As I continued to imagine air entering and leaving my vagina, I began to develop sensation in an area that is not always easy for me to feel.

"Now caress yourself—your chest, your arms, your face, your abdomen—whatever feels right to you. Express your love for your body," he said.

My hands moved slowly over my body—my breasts, my tummy, my groin area. At that point, tears streamed from my eyes.

"Now tell your body that it is beautiful. That you love it. That you will care for it." More tears flowed into my hair. It was okay to feel tender about my body, to caress it, to express gratitude for it. The estrangement I sometimes felt from a body that disappointed or embarrassed me melted away.

As I lay there touching myself, I glanced up to see the loincloth draped over the crucified Jesus. Jesus was both human and divine. He was a man and also the Son of God. Was this a sacred act, what we were doing, expressing love for the intimate parts of our bodies? Would Jesus approve? I was quite sure the priest from St. Joseph's Catholic Church in Volga, my childhood church, would not approve.

In my religious upbringing, sexuality was most often associated with mortal sin—coveting another man's wife or committing adultery. Even masturbating needed to be brought to the confessional. But now, in the midst of this sacred space, we were invited to a new, loving way of viewing ourselves, of loving our bodies

"How was that?" our marriage therapist asked at my next session. "What was that like for you?"

"I felt like crying," I said. Choking on my words, I could only demonstrate. "When I do this," I said stroking my arm, "it's like...."

It was hard to put my feelings into words. Yes, I had touched myself before, sometimes out of curiosity or a desire for pleasure. At other times just for perfunctory reasons, taking a shower or putting on clothes

But saying, "I love you," or, "I'm grateful for you," to my body, that was new, different.

"It's like my body is okay," I finally exhaled.

The therapist nodded, signaling that I was making headway.

Sensing my work was not done, I continued the counseling sessions, spilling out my story about childhood, the daily ritual of catheterization, the surprise visit to the doctor that felt invasive, the difficulty of establishing an intimate bond with a man that included sexual activity. This therapy helped me become aware of how my unique life story had played out in my relationships. I realized that love could not be built on a desire to "help" someone else change or even to change myself. Without a level of self-worth and a willingness to accept the other person in all his strengths and weaknesses, love does not have an opportunity to flourish. My marriage ended in divorce, and I moved to Des Moines to rent an apartment and begin a new life.

"It's possible my bladder will release if I have an orgasm," I learned to say sooner or later in a relationship when intimacy was increasing. But how and when to introduce this information? Explain it too early and I would likely scare off a man even before we became close enough for such involvement. Explain it too late, in the heat of the moment, and it would likely deflate the passion that had built up.

So I became a student of timing and logistics. Pay attention to that point when the outcome of the relationship and the situation was clear—we were going to make love—and explain my body's proclivities clearly and without emotion. Whip out the mattress protector and get back to the lovemaking. Men responded differently but usually it made little difference. My partner ordinarily nodded, and we got back to what we were doing.

My parents doubted whether it was possible for me to have a sexual relationship at all, I believe. After my marriage had ended, Mother, Dad and I had a brief though revealing conversation in the car.

"Diane, they told us they needed to cut the nerves to your genital area to relieve pressure on the brain," my mother said from the front seat of the car, looking straight ahead at nothing in particular and speaking in a subdued tone. "They said nature would eventually take care of things."

We were meeting in Marshalltown for Sunday dinner, as was often our custom. This time it was to note the end of my marriage. Years later, I would read about the procedure Mother described in the medical report from the University of Iowa Hospital. The neurosurgeon talked about "sacrificing a sacral nerve root" in the process of closing the spine.

"Mother and Dad, I've no regrets about all that and I know you did all you could for me," I responded. At that point I knew little of what had happened and remarkably, again, didn't ask any questions. But what was the use of challenging a decision made decades ago? I was sorry it seemed to haunt them.

"Thank you, Diane," my mother responded. The subject was closed.

In retrospect, this conversation did provide insight into what had happened shortly after my graduation from college.

"Diane, we have your room ready," Mother said, gesturing down the hall in their small ranch home.

I gasped. What is she talking about? Had they expected me to move home? I blurted out, "But, I'm moving to Chicago."

They both froze, and I tried to explain, "I've taken a job with a publishing company there." The idea that I might live independently, move away, and live a normal life appeared foreign to them.

Although they said nothing in response, they later quizzed Susie.

"Have we done something to offend Diane? Why is she moving away?"

No one in our family had left Iowa to explore the bigger world, and I was the least likely candidate for doing so, so they thought.

Perhaps they had been right. I was now back in Iowa and the permanent relationship I yearned for had eluded me. But occasionally I dated interesting men. However, something happened while dating one, in particular, that changed my attitude toward both my body and sexuality.

After dating a man for several months, sharing a friendship that reflected our mutual interests in art, music and politics, our relationship proceeded to sexual intimacy. But, to my horror, the night after our lovemaking, I discovered lesions in my genital area. Did I have herpes? And did I give this man herpes? Or did he give it to me? Horrified and anxious to find out, I arranged an appointment later that day with my doctor.

"These are herpes lesions," he said after an examination. "I'm almost positive. But we'll test the virus just to make sure."

He went on to assure me that people live with herpes, explaining the precautions that should be taken and the antiviral medications that are available to shorten the duration or suppress outbreaks.

The age of HIV and AIDS was upon us—no longer the more freewheeling 1960s, the era that baby boomers were accustomed to enjoying.

I panicked. What had I done? How could I subject my body to possible infection and even death related to AIDS? Three days later, the doctor's office called. I had shingles, not herpes. Lack of sensation in my genital area prevented the pain so common to shingles.

While the outcome was positive, this one event gave me pause. This body that had survived death in infancy due to complications from spina bifida, this body that so many — my parents, doctors, therapists — had cared for so attentively, deserved more respect. I was treating it as an instrument of pleasure, rather than a treasured gift.

Now paranoid, I arranged for a test to check for HIV. In the waiting room of the Polk County Health Department in my leather coat and business attire, I looked out of place. The people around me were young, dressed in jeans and t-shirts, some obviously down on their luck — ill, poor, distressed. Is this who I was?

The social worker called me in to reveal my results.

She smiled. "When you're done with that leather coat, I'd love to have it!"

She opened my folder and glanced over the report inside. Even a delay of thirty seconds in telling me the results seemed too long.

"The test is negative," she quietly said. "Now enjoy your day."

Leaving the modest brick building in a neighborhood I rarely frequented, crossing the parking lot that seemed way too big for this office, and getting in my car, I felt clean, released from sin, forgiven—the familiar sensation I'd had leaving confession at the Catholic church in Strawberry Point. It was time to start a new life.

Dancing at Sinsinawa revealed to me just how far I had come in inhabiting, accepting and celebrating this body with all its supposed flaws, troubled history, and insecurities. Learning the rhythms of married life and love with Jeff assured me that I had broken free from all the shame and fear that had trapped me for so long. I had started life as a child unable to take care of and control her own physical functions. I was emerging as a woman grounded in her own worth, blessed with a loving husband, and with opportunities to serve others.

"This was the highlight of the whole weekend for me," one of the guest speakers we had brought in from Chicago for the women's retreat, said. "Watching you dance brought tears to my eyes." I smiled.

8
Pain Joins
The Dance

Turning off a major highway onto a gravel road marked with a small sign, "Lake Robbins Ballroom," we traveled several miles into the darkening night without seeing any signs of life.

"This can't be right," I said to Jeff, who was driving. "Are you sure this is the right road to the ballroom?"

"I recall it's out in the middle of the country," he said. "We'll find it."

Although we were just 30 miles from Des Moines, it felt as though we had left all known landscapes and markers. But before long, we saw the distant lights, colored bulbs outlining a low-slung building, looking festive in the still, inky black countryside. As we approached, we saw people dressed in full skirts, high heels, suits and ties enter the solo door as sounds of big band music drifted out into the night.

Jeff and I had studied ballroom dancing on and off for several years, taking lessons from our friends Suzi and Jim, dance champions who had won consecutive contests in the category for older competitors.

I recalled our early lessons with Suzi and Jim, when we learned as much about ourselves and our marriage as we did about dancing. We brought very different expectations to this experience. I saw myself gliding and twirling around the floor, my skirt circling ever wider, my feet moving magically in concert with the music, my body free and young and sensuous. Jeff just hoped we would learn to dance a little better—and that it wouldn't be too much work.

"At first the pressure is on the man," our instructor said, and Jeff groaned. "He needs to learn not only the steps but also make the decisions, communicate to his partner what he wants her to do, steer clear of dancing collisions on the floor, and anticipate what he's going to do next." Then he looked pointedly at me, "And the woman must learn to follow." I was not accustomed to being a follower.

Later in our lessons our instructor said, "You two need to start dancing closer together. You are too far apart." I moved closer so our hips barely touched in wordless communication as we waltzed across the polished floor.

While we knew we were getting better, during one particularly challenging class, as we attempted to learn yet another step in the Fox Trot, we wordlessly reached the same conclusion: We weren't destined to be ballroom dance champions, nor was that our goal. With this unspoken agreement, we relaxed. We would work to become good-enough dancers.

We joined the 100-year-old Castle Club, putting on our formal attire—cocktail dresses and a tuxedo—to dance to live music in a downtown sky rise. Our dancing took us back to an era when ladies and gentleman prized graceful movement, formal social events and romantic nights out.

But that night at the Lake Robbins Ballroom, we confronted a new reality: I couldn't dance. At least not as I wanted to dance.

Neuropathy from chemotherapy and nerve pain in my feet related to the spina bifida along with growing problems with balance and stability began to make dancing difficult, if not impossible. Walking or dancing for any length of time without adequate cushioning of my feet increased the pain.

"Let's test this out," Jeff suggested in proposing we attend. "The Glenn Miller Orchestra is playing at Lake Robbins. We can try dancing, just to see."

"Okay. I'll take both my walking shoes and my dance shoes," I said, doubt already causing my voice to drop off prematurely at the end of sentences.

"Over here!" Suzi called out as she waved her hands from the other side of the ballroom. We crossed the floor and sat down at the table she had reserved for dinner. "How *are* you guys?" she asked. "Great skirt!" she added, admiring my new black and white print dancing skirt with a red ruffle.

"Good, but we're wondering whether we can dance," I began to say and then stopped. Explaining the state of my body was becoming tiresome.

Before long, the music called us to the dance floor. After putting on my thick-soled Mary Jane black walking shoes, we danced the foxtrot around the floor. Dance? This felt more like tromping. My rubber soles resisted turning on the wooden floor. I held my skirt out, as if I were twirling, and then realized it was futile.

"Jeff, don't do any turns! My feet aren't working properly," I said in a bit of panic. Fear took over—fear of losing control, of stumbling, of falling.

For the next dance, I switched to the leather-soled shoes that allowed freer movement, including pivots and turns, but pain soon crippled my feet.

"Jeff, I'm sorry, this just isn't going to work," I lamented. "Let's sit the dance out and enjoy the music."

Grief colored my perceptions of dancers on the floor as we listened to the orchestra play "In the Mood." As eighty-year-olds moved energetically and skillfully to the music, their faces told the story.

"Look at those people, ten, fifteen even twenty years older than us. Look at how happy they are, how warmly they smile at one another. That's the way I envision our retirement, Jeff. We're too young to give this up," I moaned.

"Let's not go there yet," he cautioned. "We can still dance, maybe just not the same way."

So begins another of my pain sagas, stories that include the onset of new symptoms, my struggle to address them, and then, hopefully, recovery. I wondered whether this new story would follow the all-too-familiar pattern of the past. Pain resulting from a physical ailment sidetracks me. Solutions offered by professionals disappoint me, more often than not. Discouragement and sometimes depression waylay me. Then determination rises up and eventually triumphs when I find creative new approaches for healing. But the past is the past, and those memories are only a little helpful. The prospect of starting again disheartened me. The prospect of a different ending terrified me.

So frequent has chronic pain been my companion that I've come to think of it as that unwelcome guest, the one not invited and reluctant to leave. When it arrives, I ask, "And *now*, what do you want? Is there something you're asking me to learn? I've learned more than I care to know, thank you. Isn't it time for you to go away?" Am I whining or merely responding in an understandable way? Frequently I check in with Jeff and friends for feedback.

"You are *not* whining," they reassure me. "It's natural to feel discouraged from time to time." Still, I wonder.

The fact that I can walk unassisted, let alone dance, is worth celebrating. Many people with spina bifida, particularly at my age, use wheelchairs or depend on leg braces and walkers to steady them. Yet, these limitations don't necessarily impair their lives. People of all ages with spina bifida dance, play basketball and compete in races, using their wheelchairs or other assisted devices. They remind me to be grateful for what I *am* able to do and to stop focusing on what I cannot do.

But while all this self-talk is going on, the pain demands attention, driving out efforts to be positive. It dominates my life for a time—and then leaves without explanation, giving me time to rest. At least that is the way it has worked in the past.

My childhood encompassed the usual physical activities of the young—running, bicycling, playing on gym sets, badminton, somersaults, rolling down hills and romping in leaves and snow. But in my preadolescence, the pain began in my legs.

Lying on my bed, I would cry to my dad, "It hurts so much. It shoots through my legs and into my feet. Daddy, what's wrong?"

"Honey, I don't know. Here let me massage your legs," he responded.

Not until my late thirties during the mid-1980s did a possible explanation emerge. At a national conference of the Spina Bifida Association of America I attended in Denver, a neurosurgeon reported on medical issues facing adults with spina bifida — a relatively new topic for such gatherings, added for the growing number of adults living with this birth defect.

"We're finding that the tethering of spinal cords is a problem in both children and adults. The spinal cord becomes attached to the spinal column in the womb. Then, after surgery to repair the spine, the scar tissue that forms re-tethers it. Tethering interferes with the blood supply to the spinal cord and can cause progressive deterioration — loss of bladder and bowel function, significant leg weakness, back and leg pain, and scoliosis," he said matter-of-factly.

The adults in the audience began to stir, turning to one another in confusion, asking, "Did you know about this?"

"During times of rapid growth as a child," he continued, "you may have experienced pain as your spinal cord was stretched." He then turned to the next topic, maintenance of shunt systems to drain fluid from the brain.

"Wait!" a woman called out. "Say that again. What do you mean—tethering of the spinal cord?"

"A normal spinal cord floats free in the canal, able to move up and down with growth and movement. A tethered cord is stretched in such cases, causing damage to the spinal cord," he explained.

"How often does this happen?" she questioned.

"In nearly all cases of spina bifida," he said.

Loss of bodily functions? Damage to the spinal cord? Had we survived birth, dealt with leaky bladders and weak leg muscles, only to confront these new, continuing threats? When disabling pain afflicted my back and legs a couple of years later, an MRI showed a tethered cord as a possible explanation.

"Yes, your spinal cord is tethered. It's a long tether in your case—and clean. I could chop it just like this," the local neurosurgeon said, gesturing as if he were cutting meat with an axe, "but I wouldn't recommend it right now. Let's wait and see what happens."

Not eager to have him "chop" my spinal cord, I agreed with him and returned to Dad and Susie in the waiting room outside. When I shared this information with them, Dad's jaw became slack, he bowed his head and tears formed in his eyes. He managed to save me from threatening bladder and kidney infections in childhood, but he could not save me from this.

He said then what he would say several times in our lives when a crisis hit. "I guess I can't take care of my girls any longer." To his regret, our lives were out of his control and subject to the unforeseen ups and downs of the world.

That began a year of absence from my job at the newspaper as I battled pain that prevented me both from sitting or standing for any length of time. I was forty years old, divorced, with no one in my life to take care of me if I became permanently disabled. Alone in my condo for days at a time, I listened to Aaron Copland's "Appalachian Spring" over and over again, searching for the peace and hope the music characterizes. Where were my peace and hope?

Reading about disorders of the spinal cord, I resonated with the observation that patients with such disorders begin to envision death, so central is the function of the spinal cord to every part of the body. Distraught, my body began to emulate menopause as my periods became irregular and hot flashes plagued me throughout the day. The Mayo Clinic concurred with the advice given me by the neurosurgeon. "Let's wait and see." The slightest error and the surgeon might cut a nerve that controls the legs, one of the doctors said. Also, in their experience, cutting tethered cords creates new scar tissue that re-tethers the cord.

So, I waited to see what would happen. The care of a skilled and compassionate physical therapist, water exercise, the support of my employer, patience, and Appalachian Spring got me through this yearlong ordeal without surgery.

I should have quit my job then, knowing work added to my physical problems. Meetings and desk work required long hours of sitting and ate into time for exercise and rest. Still, I resisted resigning, in part because I loved what I did and did it well, and in part because I needed health insurance and a salary to support myself.

A new problem emerged when the tethered spinal cord impaired nerves to the pelvic floor muscles. These pelvic floor muscles, the ones we sit on, had ached in an unforgiving manner for years, responding to almost anything—sitting too long, changes in the weather, or a yoga stretch that was too deep. But now one of them snapped in a deep spasm that made every minute of the day miserable. It was like sitting on a tennis ball.

I didn't talk about this pain. Most people don't know what a pelvic floor muscle is, and if they do, they don't particularly want to talk about yours. Or, so I assumed. If I told friends about this problem, I would have to tell them about the tethered cord, and then about spina bifida. I feared being viewed as "sick" or defective or incapacitated. Most of all I didn't want to be a "downer" by talking about depressing things.

Sharing my life difficulties *might* have burdened other people or at least colored our conversations and interactions, but more likely it would have opened the door to more honest, intimate relationships. People knew me only as this upbeat personality, the marketing pro, who could put a positive spin on almost anything. It was a skill I honed in childhood as I sought to convince Mother and Dad that everything was okay. They need not worry about me, I assured them.

Speculations about childhood aside, I needed to address this current problem. An osteopathic doctor who specialized in manual manipulation summed it up succinctly.

"Why are you picking on me?" he asked without a hint of humor or empathy as he reviewed my medical history, suggesting he preferred I go somewhere else for help. He knew his field well, I was told, but my referral failed to mention his inept communication style.

"This pelvic floor muscle is completely inverted," he said as he examined me. "It's twisted in a shape that will cause you a lot of pain. You need to change this, or the quality of your life will go down significantly."

In my view, it had already gone down significantly. Despite his assessment and attempts to release the spasm, nothing he tried worked. When consulting with other professionals — neurologists, physical and occupational therapists and several doctors — turned up no new ideas, I decided to visit a California holistic medical center on grounds reputed to have healing properties.

Aching from a long travel day, I pulled up in a van to Meadowlark north of Los Angeles and eyed the rundown house and surrounding out buildings skeptically. Was this a mistake, committing myself to staying here for a whole week? But soon, Dr. Evart Loomis, a handsome, exceptionally fit man in his 80s, who had founded Meadowlark in the 1930s, came out to greet everyone warmly.

"You have the run of the place. We only have a few guests this week, so make yourself at home," he said as I stepped up onto the porch with my suitcase.

Having the pick of almost any room in this main house or adjoining buildings, I chose "The Womb," a small room next to the kitchen of the house. Before the week was out I sampled dream therapy, healing touch, and massage, but it was a private session with a Qigong instructor that suggested a way forward.

"Imagine energy entering the top of your head and flowing down your spine," she instructed as we stood one morning out on the grass of the spa grounds.

The sun warmed my head, my shoulders, my whole body, and I felt myself relax. With feet planted firmly on the ground, I felt connected both with the Earth and with the sky.

"Take that energy gradually down each verte-bra of your back, releasing any tension that might be there," she continued.

"I see it! I see it," I cried out.

"What are you seeing?" she said as she stopped the visualization.

"My spinal cord," I responded. "I see it and it's alive!"

"Alive?" she said. "Tell me more."

"It's gold. It's giving off a warm glow. My spinal cord didn't die," I gasped in amazement.

To anyone else, this response would be weird and baffling, but not to her. She quietly encouraged me to continue talking with my eyes closed. I related the story of my birth, the expectation I would die, and the assumption I must have internalized that something at the core of my being did indeed die.

Each day, as I imagined energy entering the top of my head and flowing down my spine, I noticed a slight relaxing of the pelvic floor muscle. Encouraged that this practice might eventually unwind it, on the ride back to the airport, I resolved to do this visualization daily. Before I had a chance to get started, the muscle tightened up again when I returned to work. Undaunted, I returned to the practice. For an hour every day for a year, I visualized golden energy flowing down the spine and into the muscle that was knotted. Gradually electrical sensations pulsed through the affected muscle, and with more time, caused it to flutter and unwind.

Through this experience, I gained new awareness about the power of my mind to observe my body and to address physical problems through visualization. This new-found discovery raised an important question. Was I only going to engage in such healing practices in response to acute problems or would I take steps to prevent such problems by changing my life? I knew my demanding job, requiring as it did long hours of sitting doing stressful work, compounded the issues of an already compromised body.

But I wasn't ready to leave. I hung on until I was 51 and had been diagnosed with breast cancer. Finally, my body told me I had to walk away from this increasingly damaging life. There was no middle ground in my mind. Change or die, or at least become significantly disabled. With the support of Jeff, whom I had married four years earlier, I left my job.

The combination of breast cancer with spina bifida was not good news, particularly for my bones. The chemotherapy often used in treating cancer patients damages bone density. As someone with spina bifida, I was already at risk for osteoporosis. Adding to my concern was my family history. Both my parents had broken hips because of osteoporosis.

My fear was warranted. After six months of chemotherapy and seven weeks of radiation, my bone density dropped 10 percentage points. The impact of this bone loss, plunging me into osteoporosis, would become apparent within a few years. Severe buttock and leg pain prompted another MRI that showed insufficiency fractures in the sacrum.

"How did this happen?" I quizzed my doctor. "I didn't fall. I don't remember doing anything unusual or remarkable." My research showed that such fractures were most likely to occur in women in their eighties and beyond.

"The quality of the bone in your sacrum may be deficient because of spina bifida," she conjectured. "Aging also contributes. That, combined with the osteoporosis, makes you vulnerable to these fractures."

Regardless the cause, the impact was immediate and distressing. Literally unable to sit without intense pain, I quit my piano lessons, dropped out of my writing group, stopped going to concerts, movies, plays, and dinners with friends, and canceled memberships in women's groups—all activities that required sitting. Struggling to find a position other than standing or lying down, I bought a zero-gravity chair that tilted me far enough back to take the pressure off the sitz bones, the bones in the pelvis we sit on. This position lessened the pain, but disappearing from pursuits I loved led to a lonely life apart from friends.

An enthusiastic amateur pianist, I had taken lessons more than ten years as an adult at the Drake University Community School of Music. I traveled several times to the Piano Sonata, a piano camp for adults in Vermont. My Piano Club consisted of people, like me, who took their playing seriously and desired to share their music.

"Bob, I can't come any more to my piano lessons," I said to my piano teacher at the end of our lesson, putting off this conversation as long as possible. "The pain of sitting is too much for me."

"We're just halfway through the Mompou Variations on a Theme by Chopin," he said as if to underscore the importance of continuing.

"Yes, I'd love to finish them, but for now, it's just too difficult," my voice broke.

"How about Piano Camp?" he continued. "Is that still possible? And what about Piano Club?"

I turned my back to him grabbed my purse and fumbled for a tissue.

"Not now. Another time, perhaps. Right now, I need to recover. That means not sitting as much as possible," I explained. Going home, I closed up the lid of my grand piano, put away the piano books, including the Mompou Variations, and called my friend Cris in Piano Club to explain my upcoming absence.

"Come anyway," she encouraged. "You can lie down on the sofa while others play."

It was a solution I would come to accept with numerous groups—just go and then lie down while others sit. This strategy kept me somewhat connected during the years of recovery that followed. I reclined through workshops, individual sessions with my clients in spiritual direction, group meetings, and after-dinner conversations with friends.

"Do you need to lie down today?" Mary, a friend in Shalom, a spirituality group, still routinely asks when we gather monthly. "Here I have this mattress we can place on the floor, or we can give you the couch to yourself." Before long, no one seems to notice that I'm horizontal. If I need to read from a book or handout or make a point more forcefully, I prop myself up on one elbow.

Even more than breast cancer, these insufficiency fractures, resulting as they did in nerve damage, changed my life. For the next five years, I pursued various therapies and alternative approaches: water exercise, walking, physical therapy, meditation, and visualization. I became a student of my pain. Is it sharp or dull? Static or moving? Red or blue? Burning or stabbing? Noticing your pain without responding to it emotionally can reduce suffering, so the experts say. In meditating on the pain, I found it could be reduced. I still *had* pain, but I was able to distance myself from it, at least part of the time. I no longer *was* my pain, an insight that gave me some comfort.

What was difficult to replace was the joy that piano playing brought. When I play the piano, I go inside, searching for the feeling the music calls forth, and then work to bring that feeling back into my playing, even as I am learning the rhythm and technique. The beauty of the music lives in my head, inspired by renditions of these pieces played on CD by professionals and by what I sense the composer's intent to be. Playing the piano takes me into my lyrical, emotional self in a way few other involvements do. I leave the constricted, inner world of tension and pain and expand to fill a spacious world of light and joy. Even though the pain does not always disappear, it takes its place in an environment I can only call happiness.

Now, somewhat more able to sit, I currently allocate my sitting time to writing this book. Trying to do both, play the piano and write, stretches my physical capabilities. Clearly, pain has become more than just an unwelcome guest. It provides direction, what to do, what not to do. It shows me the steps to a goal, once I commit myself to a course of action. It sometimes, of necessity, takes the lead, a reality I find difficult to accept.

"Is pain running your life, or *ruining* your life?" an article in a health magazine challenges me to consider. I prefer to think of pain as a partner, not a dictator. If we work together, the outcome is better than if I take off on my own and fight reality. The body embodies its own wisdom and tells us, if we ask, what we can do to feel better. And sometimes it speaks in dramatic ways.

Through the years of dealing with cancer and then pain, I had ignored my old problem, my bladder, as increased leakage made it difficult to leave the house for more than two hours. But a dream suddenly reminded me that addressing incontinence was now a priority. In this dream, I sit at my computer in the upstairs office of our farmhouse. Suddenly a pale, thin woman dressed in a frilly, worn black and white servant outfit barely covering her frame appears at my door. She carries a serving tray laden with drinks intended for whom I'm not sure. She appears ready to collapse.

"Who are you?" I ask, surprised.

"I'm your bladder," she says with a touch of cynicism and resignation.

She didn't need to spell it further. I got the message: "Take some action! I've had it! I can't hold up much longer."

The next day, I thumbed through the yellow pages for yet another urologist, someone new with a solution for this leaky bladder I hadn't tried. Drugs had not worked. More frequent catheterization had only a modest effect. I had avoided surgery, but was now the time to consider it?

At that time, the newspaper reported on a young woman who had started a new practice in urology in Des Moines. I called her office and scheduled an appointment for two weeks later.

She proposed a unique yet counter-intuitive solution. Do a surgery, in this case a bladder sling, which made it *impossible* for me to go to the bathroom, except with a catheter. Rather than focus on making it easier to empty the bladder, make it more difficult. The advantage, she said, would be that leakage would be reduced, perhaps eliminated. Always having a catheter with me would be imperative.

While I worried a bit about this restriction (what if I forgot or ran out of catheters?), the potential for correcting incontinence convinced me to give it a try. I was a dancer, after all, used to surrendering to someone else's lead and ready to take two steps back in order to take three steps forward. The surgery worked and finally, at age 62, life offered me new freedom.

Every case of spina bifida is unique. No approach is right for everyone. Was it a mistake, I ask, now in my sixties, not to have surgery to release the tethered cord? Would it have made a positive difference? My doctors continue to advise against it. "You're a relatively high-functioning adult," they say, "and the risks outweigh the benefits. You've made it this far. Why take a chance?"

As the evening of dancing continued at Lake Robbins, we watched our friends leave the dinner table to foxtrot, waltz, rumba, and swing— all our favorite dances. Around 9 p.m. we decided it was time to go home.

"Suzi, we're leaving," I said, putting away my

dance shoes. "It's just too hard tonight for me with these sore feet."

"Take care of her," Suzi said to Jeff as she gathered us both up in a hug. "And take care of one another."

On the way home, I stared out into the dark night, this time pondering what a life without dancing would be like.

"I'm so sad," my voice cracked and I couldn't go on. Jeff reached over and stroked my shoulder. I tried to continue, "Not just for me but for both of us."

"I know, honey," he whispered.

"What will replace dancing for us if I can't do this? It's one of our favorite things to do."

"We can still dance," Jeff said, consoling me. "We can go back to the shuffle and two-step of our courting days. Remember what we used to call 'slow dance,' swaying to the music with our arms around one another?"

"Those were romantic times, you're right," I responded, attempting a more light-hearted tone. "We'll just have to get out of the way of our friends who are doing all the fancy moves around us."

I smiled. Yet, I knew that from now on I would likely have two partners, pain and Jeff, competing for my attention, one dragging me toward the sidelines, and the other leading me with a firm hand back into the dance of life.

9

FALLING OUT OF STEP

My stepson Tim and I were destined to be an-
tagonists. He suffered from mental illness.
I lived with physical illness. He floundered in
addressing his issues. I fought to survive mine.
He struggled to control his mind. I struggled to
control my body. Too often these contrasts divided, rather than united us. I understand these
differences now and also the fact that we both
struggled with something shameful to talk about.

One event has taken particular poignancy in
light of what was soon to happen. It's Sunday
evening, May 18, 2014. Tim has just arrived for
our weekly dinner together with Jeff and his sister Ann. Tim's weight gain and slumping posture
convey depression, a dramatic change from just
two years ago when he flashed a big smile as we
photographed him stir frying vegetables in our
kitchen. Yet his hair is neatly cut, and his clothes
are clean. Buoyant in mood just minutes before,
I clamp down on my enthusiasm as he walks in,
trying to respect his mood, an accommodation I

will come to see as unwise and unnecessary. Remaining silent in the face of his silence only perpetuates our family's dilemma.

Despite the fact that we've suggested he come early to help prepare the meal, he arrives at the last minute, mumbles a hello and sits down, waiting for us to serve his food. We have prepared his favorite meal—chicken parmesan and green beans.

"How are you, Tim?" I ask.

"Okay," he responds and then eats his meal in silence. He cleans up his plate and reaches for seconds on the green beans, although he reassures us time and time again that he feels no pleasure anymore in eating—or anything else.

Jeff, Ann and I carry on a conversation without him in an effort to simulate normalcy.

"Did you read about that new Indian restaurant opening in Clive?" Ann asks.

"I heard about it. Has anyone you know been there?" I respond.

"No, but the review in the paper sounded good," Ann says.

"Let's go sometime," Jeff says.

The superficial conversation continues, but the fact we are not enjoying this time together becomes apparent. Jeff's voice drops to almost a whisper, his head down. I compensate by speaking louder with unwarranted cheerfulness. Ann jumps in to suggest new topics when neither of us speaks. Anger, causing my stomach to churn, rises into my chest and then into my throat. I can no longer resist speaking up.

"It would be nice if you would talk more, Tim." (I fail to see the irony in me being the one to expect someone else to talk more.)

Jeff and Ann pull back slightly from the table. The drama begins.

"You think it's easy for me to talk? Like you can just say, 'Talk, Tim,' and I will?" he retorts, his face getting red as his eyes bore into mine.

"You have no idea what my condition is like," he continues. "My condition makes it impossible to talk."

"You're talking now," I challenge him, knowing what's coming.

"F..... you. I'm out of here." Tim stands up and grabs his jacket.

Jeff gets up to hug Tim, who responds stiffly and storms out, and then he rejoins us at the table.

"Did you need to do that?" Jeff confronts me, impatience twisting his normally calm face into a grimace. "You know the response you'll get."

"I'm tired of pretending everything is okay. Our conversations over dinner are strained. We're faking it, trying to keep everything smooth. Is it too much to expect that Tim participate in dinner—help prepare it or talk when he's here?"

By now, dinner has ended prematurely. Jeff begins to clean up the dishes. Ann helps. I put away the uneaten food.

"This is my last attempt to keep Tim somewhat connected to the family," Jeff explains. "Other than this one evening each week, we have no way of communicating with him."

"But this is not communicating in any meaningful way. Tim is totally in control. We play by his rules by accepting his silence and pretending everything is fine." I'm venting now, not only the frustration of this one evening, but also the resentment of years of trying to relate to Tim.

"Jeff, I can't do this anymore," I say after Ann leaves. "I've given up on the possibility that Tim and I will ever have a good relationship, but is it too much to ask that he be civil?"

Sinking back into his chair, Jeff sighs. We've been at this point before. "Think about this, Diane," he counsels. "You've struggled with controlling your bladder all your life. Tim can't control his mind. Isn't that much worse?"

The next morning, submerged in the warm water of the swimming pool downstairs in our condominium, I search my conscience, questioning whether I have lost my capacity for compassion. Is that a fair comparison—that my issues of control pale in comparison to Tim's? Is it less humiliating to have an accident at school in front of your adolescent friends than to find yourself unable to form relationships because of a mental health condition? Or is that even the relevant question?

The warm water, broken into glass-like crystals from the sun pouring through full-length patio doors, supports me as I try to put myself back to those days when I truly felt out of control, when I was frightened, embarrassed, even angry that I couldn't do what everyone around me did so naturally. A particular example surfaced immediately.

O ne day in fifth grade during a history test, I felt especially anxious about whether I could hold the urine in my increasingly full bladder. I worked through the test questions: *The event marking the beginning of World War II. The leader of Great Britain during the war.* It was hard to concentrate. Twenty more minutes before the end of class.

The act bringing the United States into the war. The date of the landing of U.S. troops at Normandy. I glanced up at the clock. Only five minutes have lapsed. Fifteen more to go. I looked around me. Everyone's head was down, focused on the test. In the middle of the room, second row from the door, I resisted the urge to flee, leaving my test paper behind.

In one terrifying moment, my bladder collapsed and urine streamed around me, creating a puddle under my desk and into the aisle. There was no hiding this. Yet I persisted in answering the questions: *The countries part of the Alliance. The countries supporting Hitler.* God, help me.

The bell rang. I got up, skirt dripping, handed in my paper and headed out the door, glancing at no one and explaining nothing. Down two flights of stairs, out the same back door my mother and I entered that first day of school, through the stands of cottonwood trees and into the back door of our white bungalow.

Before long I was crying and screaming. My mother needed no explanation, seeing my wet skirt. We removed my clothes, and I changed into something dry, flinging myself on the bed.

"I can never go back," I cried out. "I can't face them again!"

Head buried in a pillow, my cries became muffled. Mother brought out my grandmother's Russian Orthodox Bible, a thick black-covered book with gold-edged pages and strange characters I couldn't read. My first-grade picture was stuck in the middle of the pages.

"Grandma used to pray for you," Mother said, showing me the picture, but it was of no comfort. Grandma wasn't there, and she couldn't undo the events of the last hour. My mother said little. Perhaps this was her worst fear for me too. How could this have been prevented? Did she wonder about this? I don't know.

What I did know was that that night was the spring choral concert. Should I go? Stay home? Would my family go with me? I washed my face trying to get rid of the redness and changed my clothes once again. I went. Alone. My parents stayed home. I knew how to pretend that everything was okay. That was what I did.

I sang the songs. "Shenandoah, " "Tennessee Waltz," "Catch a Falling Star." An alto, I stood to the left in the front row. Were people looking at my skirt? The floor? In an improbable daydream, I imagined no one noticed my accident. I tried to focus on the words of the songs, the ones we had practiced for weeks.

After the concert, Loretta, a girl in my class, called out in front of several other students, "There's Betsy Wetsy!" I momentarily froze in place, studying her face. Was she attempting to make me feel even more foolish than I already did? Making a little joke to help me feel better and rejoin my friends? Was this the beginning of teasing and taunting by the other kids? I forced my mouth into a false smile, said nothing and walked out of the room.

No one ever mentioned the event again. My teacher didn't comment, the kids didn't tease me, and my mother didn't ask me about the choral concert or aftermath of this accident. Like so many such events of my life, it was submerged in a pool of shame.

Memories of that traumatic childhood event quickly brought up other distressful incidents that continued until adulthood. Doing a leisurely backstroke in the pool, the water holding me protectively, I became a witness at that moment to a life difficult in some respects, but a life I survived.

Marching in a parade with my students from my high school journalism class during my campaign for the Iowa Senate. I have to go to the bathroom — now. I dash to a house along the parade route and ask a startled homeowner if I can use her bathroom. She agrees. I run to catch up with the parade.

Traveling in a five-seat airplane with no bathroom with four other political party executives to an event at which I am to speak. What will happen if my bladder lets out in mid-flight? Imagine the mess, the embarrassment, and the conundrum about what to do when we arrive. Please, God, help me.

Sitting on a dais at a Gannett company-wide meeting at which I am to facilitate a panel introducing a major new marketing initiative. I worry about an accident but the mental challenge of listening to the panel and asking questions blocks out my fear

Wishing I had not had that cup of coffee minutes before the musical performance is to begin. I am in the middle of a long row of seats at the Civic Center, and the lights dim. It's too late to leave. Can I keep my mind on the show and not my bladder? I find it difficult to concentrate on the lyrics and the music.

Declining to go with my friends on a canoe

trip because it will mean two hours without access to a bathroom. I say "no," even though I want to go.

Sightseeing in Savannah with Jeff on a tour bus with no restroom. I can't finish the tour without leaking, but I can't get off the bus and get back to our B & B. We stop to tour a historic church and I'm stunned to see a restroom right inside the door. Usually, church restrooms are well hidden. Thank you, God.

Waiting to play my solo at the Piano Sonata, the piano camp for adults. When will my name be called? I went to the bathroom a half hour ago at break, but still my turn to perform has not come up. Should I go again, and chance missing the calling of my name, or should I wait? The question distracts me from focusing on the recital and adds to my growing anxiety about performing.

In these moments of recollection, I connect with Tim's probable distress, his isolation, and his fear of trusting himself and others in social situations. There's no one to talk with. No one to share my fears with. Only dreadful consequences to imagine. It's impossible to experience pleasure in any given moment if you're hounded by prospects of what might happen next.

My heart softens with the healing waves of the pool, created by my swimming. Tim's face comes to mind. Although I don't pretend to understand what he's going through, I sense his loneliness, his fear of speaking up, his bewilderment about how to make his way in the world. Could I have survived my years of living with incontinence if my ability to use my mind, to reflect on what was happening, to console myself after particularly difficult incidents, and to find solace in my piano and books had been impaired?

Leaving the pool and going upstairs to shower, I reflect on the fact that during my career as a teacher, political consultant, and marketing executive, rarely did my fears result in the disastrous accidents I envisioned. And in those cases when those accidents occurred, often an unexpected grace to ease the pain descended on me.

The Coliseum lights dim. The swell of circus music fills the cavernous space. The spotlight turns on me as I walk out in front of five thousand people to welcome the Moscow Circus as the Register's sponsor of the event. My bladder has just collapsed, and my shoes squish as I walk.

My planning was less than perfect tonight. Heather, the twelve-year-old girl the Big Sister/Little Sister program matched me with, and I decided to make an evening of it. We ate dinner at McDonald's, her choice. At that point, I should have used the restroom, but I trusted I could go just before the event for optimum timing.

What I hadn't planned on was the congestion surrounding Hilton Coliseum. As hundreds of cars clog the entry to the parking lots, we drive around for 30 minutes looking for a spot to leave the car. As my bladder begins to feel overextended, my anxiety grows. When we can't find a parking spot, I pull up to the Coliseum in a restricted parking zone, tell Heather we need to hurry and together we dash for the door. I make my appeal.

"Can we come in? I need to go…," I say to the guard without spelling out why. Surely he can guess.

"This is not an official entrance. We can't let you in here," he responds. Heather watches with interest as I give my best "please, help me" look to the guard.

"I really, really need to use the restroom. I can't wait," I tell him, spelling things out more specifically this time.

He opens the door, steps aside and says nothing. Heather and I dash in, but it's too late. My bladder spills urine over my panties, pad, pantyhose, and navy flats, soiling my skirt as well. Now a new strategy must be developed. How to deal with wet clothes less than 20 minutes before I'm to appear on stage. Heather watches with interest as I remove my pants and pantyhose in the restroom, dump them in the wastebasket and empty out my shoes.

"Okay, Heather, we're ready now," a fact she accepts without criticism or question. "I'll find a place for you to sit, do my thing in front of the audience, and then rejoin you, okay?"

"Okay!" she says, more interested in the Moscow Circus than me at this point.

Now outside the entrance to the arena, I hear the music. Taking a deep breath, I stride in with slightly exaggerated movements, which I hope will be interpreted as confidence, and call out "Welcome, Ladies and Gentlemen!" in my best circus mistress voice, the one I've never tested before. The next minutes blur in my mind as I repeat the brief speech intended to convey the *Register*'s commitment to its readers through sponsorship of this event.

From a distance, it surely won't be apparent my skirt is wet, I hope. I'm wearing a hot pink jacket with generous shoulder pads, the better to stand out before a crowd. A clown comes over and begins to examine my jacket. Soon he's picking up the shoulder pads and dropping them to the delight of the crowd. I ignore him and continue my spiel. He dances around me, delighted to poke fun at this businesswoman surrounded by elephants, scantily dressed performers and all manners of hoops, swings, and balance beams. My responsibility over, I head to the row of seats where Heather is sitting.

"You were funny!" she giggled as I reach her. "He kept picking up and dropping your jacket!"

Having been given some compassion toward Tim, I ask the question: Why has a young man with mental health issues, deserving of my understanding, been so able to push my buttons over the years? Shouldn't a reasonably mature, capable person like me be able to be less reactive?

When Jeff and I started dating, Tim lived primarily with his mother but stayed with Jeff every other weekend during the school year and summer vacation. We incorporated Tim into our relationship almost immediately. At age twelve, Tim could be playful and fun, performing his magic tricks and acrobatics for me, including this amazing feat where he walks up the side of a wall. But he also had a short fuse.

"I don't like this chicken," Tim fumed over dinner.

"Well, that's what we have, so eat what you want," Jeff said calmly, experienced in the dynamics that were about to unfold.

"I won't eat it," Tim screamed and began to rage at his dad.

"Then don't eat it. But you can't stay at the dining room table and behave in this way," Jeff responded.

I admired Jeff's firmness. He wasn't about to give in to a temper tantrum.

Then Tim made an unexpected entry into our life on a more permanent basis on the night we returned from our honeymoon, in 1995, three years later. We got out of the cab after a blissful week in Savannah at a historic bed and breakfast. Jeff and I strode into our home, purchased a year earlier, our arms filled with suitcases, hats, and shopping bags. The phone rang. It was Tim.

"Where are you, Tim?" I heard Jeff say, portraying that sober face with its intense searching eyes I have come to know all too well. After a while, Jeff requested more firmly. "Tim, you need to tell me where you are." After a few minutes, it was apparent the conversation was going nowhere. "Tim, I'll call you back. Give me a number where I can reach you."

Jeff turned to me. "Tim has run away from home. He doesn't want to live with his mother anymore. He says he won't tell us where he is unless we agree that he can come live with us."

I'd been mulling over the possibility of Tim living with us, wanting to reach out to this boy who, I felt, needed a more loving home. But I hadn't anticipated it would happen this quickly.

"I'm okay with having him here," I assured Jeff. "I had envisioned we'd have time to get settled and used to each other before we invited him to join us. But, do what you think is best."

Jeff was hesitant. "I don't like the circumstances under which this is happening. Starting with a demand like the one Tim is making is not healthy. 'Agree that I can live with you or else.' That doesn't feel right," he said.

"Yes, but what will happen if we say 'no'?" I respond. "Where will he stay tonight?"

In retrospect, Jeff's hesitation was well founded. That night began four difficult years of Tim's living with us—years characterized by rage, destruction of property, drug use, and an evolving personal vendetta against me. When I played the piano, Tim slammed doors in protest. When I asked him to pick up his dirty laundry from the front hall, he punched holes in walls. When I tried to be helpful, he rejected my overtures. One day stands out:

"Keep your fucking hands off my laundry," Tim yelled at me.

"I put it in the dryer to be helpful," I responded.

"I don't need or want your help," he barked back.

Hours later, sitting in our favorite sunroom right off the kitchen, I talked with Jeff about what had happened with the laundry.

"I was just trying to help out. He's totally out of control. His angry outbursts are out of line," I said, as I held my head and cried. In just three days, I was scheduled to have a mastectomy. My future was looking uncertain with cancer that doctors had been unable to see in the mammogram but confirmed with a biopsy.

"I can't do this anymore," I sobbed. "I can't go through surgery wondering if it's safe to return home."

"What do you want me to do?" Jeff's voice was barely audible.

Rarely had my dear husband looked so defeated, so empty, so without answers. Counseling was, after all, his profession. Helping people with emotional problems was his gift. But the therapy Tim had done with a colleague of Jeff's had not worked.

"Tim needs to move out," I said reluctantly. "There's no other way. This situation isn't going to change." Jeff didn't respond, so I pressed on. "I need your support right now. I'm afraid."

The next day, Jeff relocated Tim to a nearby apartment, ending the daily confrontations at home but not solving the underlying issues. Tim would go on to drop out of high school, move in with an older woman with drug abuse issues, and exhibit suicidal tendencies. All this time, Jeff worked with him to stabilize his life and arrange for psychiatric help. With Jeff's encouragement, Tim eventually got his GED.

In 2003, when Jeff and I moved to our farmhouse in Carlisle, the home of our dreams on a peaceful eight-acre plot, Tim again approached us about moving in. Recently released from the mental health unit of the hospital, Tim was clearly unstable. How could we turn him away? On the other hand, how could we let him in? Everything within me cried, "No! Not again!" Against all reason, I knew I would never play the piano again. Tim's door slamming would prevent that — or at least remove my pleasure in this pursuit. Every day Jeff would leave for work in Des Moines and Tim, unemployed, would be with me — in my personal space, in my workspace, in my life.

"How would you like it if you had to take Tim

to work every day with you?" I asked Jeff, not expecting an answer to a question designed to increase his discomfort. Crossing my arms defiantly, I refused to talk about it further. But, the old question arose, the one we had faced eight years earlier upon returning from our honeymoon. Where will Tim go tonight? What if we turn him away and he kills himself?

"You need to take him in," Aaron, Tim's brother, urged, wanting to support his younger brother during this crisis. "He needs to know he's part of a family that cares for him."

Easy enough for you to say, I fumed to myself, you who are four hours away living in an apartment.

"Not here, not in our house," I pleaded.

But finally relenting, I agreed to allow Tim to move in with us until the issue could be resolved. The old behaviors resumed. Though he had his own guest suite, he used our bathroom without permission, lounged on our bed while talking on the phone, and in general crossed every boundary that I had established in my mind. Then I thought of the little cottage we had on our property. I took a deep breath, trying to convince myself that I was not being heartless, trying to tell myself that someone needed to set some boundaries, trying to tell myself that love sometimes had to be tough.

"If Tim is going to stay here, it's not in this house," I told Jeff. "He can live in the cottage, but he comes here to our home as a visitor, not as a resident. I'm willing to help him, but I'm not willing to live like a hostage in my own space."

Jeff was clearly torn, wanting to help Tim, wanting to be responsive to Aaron, wanting to listen to me. What was clear to me was that if boundaries were to be set protecting me from what felt like an invasion, I needed to set them.

With this decided, Tim moved into the cottage and began a relatively peaceful two years of living near to us and going back to school at the local community college.

"Here's my latest paper," he said to me one evening. Enrolled in a composition class, the teacher challenged the students to write eight essays during the term. The latest was on his trip to India to participate in his brother Aaron's wedding to Saraswati.

"Tim, this is wonderful. I love all the detail you've included about the food, the dress, Saraswati's home, the ceremony itself. You have a real gift for setting the scene of a story," I said, genuinely encouraged by the work he was doing.

"My teacher loved the last essay," he responded. "She gave me an 'A.' Do you have any suggestions for improving this one?"

We continued our conversation as I asked him if he'd like to stay for dinner and help get it ready. The picture we took that night of him cooking, a radiant smile on his face as he turned to face the camera, was one of my favorites. We would snap others much like it, a handsome young man, animated by being with his family and feeling a rare moment of peace and happiness. Tim asked that we use a picture of his cooking in our farmhouse kitchen for his obituary the week before he took his life by suicide.

When Tim moved out after graduating from the community college to go to Iowa State University, I cried, much to my surprise.

"Tim's leaving tomorrow," I said to Jeff, my voice cracking. "We need to help him pack up."

"You'll miss him, won't you?" Jeff responded. "I will too. This time has been the happiest time *we've* had with him and the happiest time *I've* had with him."

Who would have guessed that our relationship with Tim could deepen to this extent and then dissipate over the next four years as mental health problems claimed his brain's ability to function?

Tim has been gone only three months as I write this in August of 2014, so it's difficult to process all that has happened in light of his decision to take his own life. Jeff and I continue to talk through our grief.

"My need for boundaries and my fear of violation caused me to be too reactive to Tim at times and made developing a relationship with him difficult," I acknowledge. "Maybe my childhood experiences played into this, the fact that I didn't even control my own body growing up. I wish I had loved Tim more fully and more boldly, despite his behavior."

"I should have been firmer in setting boundaries. Sometimes I stick to a course of action that's not working just because of my tendency to persist against all reason," Jeff responds.

"What should we have done differently?" we both ask, knowing that this question is usually not answerable after a suicide.

"I should have gotten him more serious help earlier in life. I didn't recognize the depth of his problems," Jeff says.

"True, but even the psychiatrist, who saw Tim shortly before he took his own life, said that early signs of schizophrenia are difficult to recognize in teens," I console Jeff, "if that's what his diagnosis truly was." To this day, we're still not sure. We bemoan the lack of mental health services for the seriously ill.

We miss Tim. I even miss our Sunday night dinners, strained as they were. After nearly twenty years of having him in our married life, all we can do is pick up the pieces and re-envision our life moving forward. The Sunday dinners continue with Ann.

"Wait, we only need three placemats," I remind myself.

"It's strange not having him come in the door," Jeff says.

"I miss his phone calls," Ann says. "He'd call me sometimes so as to not keep bothering you."

We take comfort in the arrival of another grandchild soon, as well as our grandson Soma.

"We'll have someone new to love," I say.

"And we have one another, our sisters, our friends, our time together in retirement," Jeff says.

Eventually, we'll feel more deeply the emotions these statements are designed to engender, but for now we do our best just to keep up the conversation.

10
JESUS COMES CALLING

My spiritual path has zigzagged through-out the decades. I've been a conscientious Catholic girl who loved Jesus, a fallen-away Catholic exploring the liberal 60s, a new-ager checking out California spas, a careerist who largely abandoned religion altogether, a practitioner of Qigong with its emphasis on connecting with universal chi, a cancer patient facing death and surrendering the outcome of treatment to God, and, now, someone Jesus wanted back. Or so it seemed one morning, as I awakened to find him in my bedroom.

But this Jesus wasn't the Jesus of my child-hood, this man who appeared not once but twice, filling the room with light and jolting me awake. Tall, muscular, commanding, his body held me captive if only for a second or two. At that mo-ment, I no longer wanted to resist him, this em-bodied Jesus, this masculine Jesus, this authori-tative Jesus who called to me by reaching out his hand. Was he asking me to dance?

His hair was golden brown and his dress—wheat and rose-colored robes—resembled the pictures and statues I had seen over the years. But his shoulders were broader, his eyes piercing, his confident posture thrilling.

As I write this, my feminist, liberal self shrinks in embarrassment. My God is female, or so I think. The persistent male language of the Christian liturgy offends me. Yet, here I am swooning over God in male form. And I'm no Jesus freak, the kind who stands on street corners proclaiming her born-again status and calling others to come to their Savior. Yet, here I am, unable to deny that Jesus came calling.

When he first appeared that moment before dawn, I sat straight up in bed. Bright light flooded the room. Then he disappeared. "Is that you, Jesus?" I whispered. He came back, bringing again the intense golden glow that surrounded not only him but also me.

I had heard of such phenomena: people, usually regarded as saints, seeing mystical images leading them to devote their lives to God in nunneries, to lead their countries in war as St. Joan of Arc did, or to perform miraculous feats of healing. But I was no saint. In the Gospels, however, Jesus was more often than not hanging out with sinners. That's probably what he was doing that morning. It was 2006, seven years out from my cancer diagnosis and I was feeling more confident about my future. Was Jesus inviting me to my next challenge?

Glancing out the bedroom window and seeing only a hint of pink above the prairie behind our house, I knew the sun would not come up for a half hour or so.

Jeff left for work early that day, as he often does. At 5:30 a.m. the time was not right to call anyone else. Who would I call anyway? And what would I say? That I had just seen Jesus? Most people would laugh, say nothing or change the subject.

In a dream the next night, I am floating down a fast-moving river in a canoe with no oars. "It's too late to go back to shore," I hear a voice from an indeterminate location say. "That's okay," I respond, relaxing and letting the river carry me. The next morning I awake to see a red poster with black lettering flash before my eyes. "Women for the Earth," it says. The poster called for action. What kind of action? I wasn't sure.

The meaning of Jesus' appearance continued to hound me. Unable to escape his insistent presence, I told my spiritual direction group what had happened. We came together monthly to talk about our lives and discern how the Spirit was working in them.

"I saw Jesus in my bedroom a couple times two weeks ago," I said. Their questions told me either they were incredulous or jealous.

"Why haven't I seen him?" one woman asked.

"Are you sure? This may have just been a dream," another said.

"Perhaps it was nothing," I acknowledged, "but it seemed real enough."

"Now don't apologize for what you've witnessed," the leader of the group, an experienced spiritual director, cautioned. "Claim your experience."

Reluctant after the initial response from the group, I continued, this time with a greater sense of urgency.

"I'm feeling hounded by him. I'm not ready to devote my life to God." Devoting my life to God equaled giving up the pleasures of my life—food, friends, travel, and clothes. I was no ascetic. We now lived on a beautiful acreage in a spacious house with a Steinway piano in our living room. And a vacation to Italy in the works. I was an enthusiastic shopper who rarely came home empty handed.

"Are you aware that you used the word 'hounded'?" the leader of our group asked.

"No, did I say 'hounded?'" I responded. "Why is that important?"

"Read the 'Hound of Heaven,' " she advised. Soon two copies were in the mail, one from her and one from another group member. The poet, Francis Thompson, describes his flight from God.

"I fled Him down the nights and down the days

I fled Him down the arches of the years
I fled Him down the labyrinthine ways
Of my own mind, and in the midst of tears
I hid from him, and under running laughter."

Had I been fleeing from God? Had I been hiding?

When I was a child, I loved Jesus, that gentle big brother of a young man with golden brown hair reaching below his ears and kindly eyes beckoning me to sit on his lap and tell him my concerns. Jesus became my confidante. I could tell him things no one else in my life would understand, or so I thought, and things I was afraid to tell anyone else.

"Help me through this class," I prayed, when my fear of an accident loomed.

"Please don't let them notice my diaper," I implored, when they began requiring a shower after gym class.

"Will a boy ever want to be with me?" I wondered, taking my concern to Jesus.

My relationship with this kind young man expressed itself most clearly at bedtime. Praying with Jesus in mind, not a more amorphous God, I recited this common childhood prayer:

"Now I lay me down to sleep, I pray the Lord my

soul to keep. If I shall die before I wake, I pray the Lord my soul to take. Amen."

Jesus became my protector against the Catholic Church. When the priest of our little churches in Wadena or Volga reminded us we could go to Hell for missing Mass and spoke of our inherently sinful nature, I glanced at the statue of Jesus on the altar and wondered if he felt as uncomfortable as I did. Burn in eternal damnation for deciding to stay home one Sunday morning? Whether it was that threat of punishment or my parents' inherently obedient nature, we never missed one service during my childhood unless a blizzard closed the gravel roads through the hills we traveled to church.

The little stone church in Volga was cold and drafty in the winter. The grates immediately behind the statues of Jesus and Mary, flanking either side of the altar, were meant to let in heat. They held a more sinister image for me. I was convinced that was where Purgatory was. Some day I would die and be held captive behind those metal bars until it was time to go to Heaven. I hoped Jesus would keep an eye out on me if that happened. I prayed indulgences fervently, hoping to reduce the days I would spend there.

Although the Catholic Church's conditions for granting indulgences (remission of punishment for time spent in Purgatory) were far more complex than I understood at the time, what I picked up was that if I prayed certain prayers, I could earn "time off" from my stay in this place between Heaven and Hell. Often prayers would specify how many days one could accumulate. How many days did I knock off my stay with this prayer? I don't recall, but I tallied up an impressive number by reciting this prayer several times a day.

So, all through my childhood, I prayed:

"I beseech Thee, through Thy infinite Goodness, grant that my name be engraved upon Thy Heart, for in this I place all my happiness and all my glory, to live and to die as one of Thy devoted servants."

Then, as I approached my teen years, another concern emerged. Was God calling me to become a nun? I didn't want to wear a black robe, give up the prospect of marriage and live what appeared to be a joyless life.

"Will I go to Hell if God calls me to be a nun and I don't respond?" I asked one of the nuns after our summer school Catechism class.

"You probably won't go to Hell, but you'll be placed on a lower rung of Heaven than if you had followed God's direction," she explained.

I sighed. No longer did I need to be concerned only about whether I would go to Heaven or Hell; now the worry would be about my rank in Heaven—high or low? But thankfully all this speculation became too much for me and much less interesting than the life opening to me as a teenager. Like most girls my age, boys, homecoming parades, clothes, my school classes and activities occupied my days. Once every couple of months, we went to Confession in Strawberry Point, choosing a church other than the one we regularly attended to avoid confronting the priest we knew too well. Then I worried about things like, "Have I had impure thoughts?" and, "Have I been honest in my dealings with others?"—the questions on the Catholic guide for examination of conscience. But once "cleansed of sin," I went back to the life I was living, however perfect or imperfect it might have been.

In the early morning hours of that summer day, lying in bed recalling childhood memories, waiting for my breathing and racing mind to slow after my mystical encounter with Jesus, I began to wonder whether I had abandoned my friend Jesus somewhere along the way from adolescence to adulthood.

My Christian faith teaches me that the Spirit that incarnates our bodies is eternal and that resurrection follows death. We are more than our bodies, yet we are given the gift of our bodies so that we might fully experience God's created world and do God's work. Was Jesus' appearance there to remind me of these beliefs?

Resting in bed, with the sun now bouncing its light off the walls facing the east windows, my cat Percey purring contentedly at the end of the bed, I rejected this possibility. Jesus didn't need to come back to remind me of what I could read in any number of the books on the shelves of our living room. Was the fact that Jesus was looking particularly well—robust and handsome—a clue? This possibility enticed me—Jesus as lover, as friend, as partner, someone who wanted me, all of me. My body tingled at the prospect. Here was God in human form—here was Jesus—asking me to engage with him.

Or was this a call to activism? Was I being recruited in support of God's desire to feed the hungry, protect the earth, and give hope to lost souls? Yes, yes, and yes. The most commanding message of the Gospels for me has always been, "feed my sheep." I take it literally, not only taking food to shelters, but also offering guidance to people seeking greater meaning and purpose in life through the program I had co-founded, Tending Your Inner Garden®. But, Jesus didn't need to visit me that morning to remind me of what I already knew. We are brother and sisters to one another in a world with unspeakable pain.

So, why had he come?

Seven years earlier, breast cancer had forever changed my life in many ways and most especially my relationship to God. It brought me back to church, a Lutheran faith community in downtown Des Moines with an active community outreach effort, dynamic preacher, and a stellar music program. The unique timing of my cancer diagnosis, coming as it did on the Summer Solstice, led me to a focus on the seasons of the year as most clearly celebrated in Native American spirituality.

Summer provided an opportunity to grow in knowledge, as I researched breast cancer, talked with survivors and explored both conventional and alternative modes of treatment. In the fall, I decided to let go of my job at the *Register*, a bold move considering it would mean giving up early retirement benefits available in only three years. But it was during winter, with all visible signs of life now dead, when I was challenged to face the reality that, now, it was just cancer and me. Gone was the daily cascade of casseroles and cards designed to help me through the initial shock of the diagnosis, gone were the daily self-administered injections intended to bolster my immune system, gone was the chemotherapy treatment designed to kill errant cells. But in the bleakness of this aloneness, a new possibility for healing opened up.

"You're cured," the oncologist said, after my six months of chemotherapy.

"Who knows if I'm cured?" I said with hesitation, doubting anyone can ever offer such a conclusive answer. "I'm feeling apprehensive."

"That's because we're cutting the umbilical cord," he conjectured.

The umbilical cord? Those tubes that connected me to red, clear and golden liquids in vials attached to IV lines, those drugs that often produced nausea, pain, and sleeplessness? That hardly seemed like my connection to the essence of life, yet I did feel panic in discontinuing my regular treatment sessions.

"What comes next?" I asked, "You're cutting me loose but to what?"

"We'll keep an eye on you, do some tests every six months. Now go enjoy your life," he instructed, picking up his charts, patting me on the back and going out the door.

Later that day as I sat in the rust-colored wingback chair in our sunroom, eyeing the shimmer on the crust that had now formed on the snow, thinking about my doctors' final words—"We will do tests every six months"—a depression began descending. Waiting? Doing nothing? I began pacing.

Then these words spontaneously came to mind: "God, my future, my death or my life is in your hands. Whatever you decide is okay with me. I'd prefer to live, of course. Life holds so much appeal, but I trust you to know what's best."

God didn't give me cancer and God didn't dictate the outcome, but yet I knew God was with me in this health crisis. Knowing that, feeling that, gave me a growing sense of peace and even an acceptance of death that had been missing in my life. With Stage III cancer and the surgeon's projection of the recurrence of the cancer at 50 percent, I knew not to take survival for granted.

A dream a few nights later told me something

had shifted in my heart. It opened with this startling image. Death, a Darth Vader-like figure, clothed in black, peered through the glass in our front door, as if to say, "I'm not going away." His nose pressed against one of the panes. He did not intend to allow me to escape.

What to do? Run to the back door and jump in the car? No, he would be there too. Tell him firmly that I intended to survive this cancer and he could just go visit some other house? He didn't appear easily persuadable. Reason with him. Say, "Come back in six months or a year. Then we'll know better what my chances are." That sounded weak, even fearful, not confident,

I invited him in.

"Everyone else is here. My sisters, my friends, my pastor. You might as well join the group. Here, have a seat in the living room," I said. At that moment, the air filled my chest and abdomen again. I could breathe more easily. Then I saw him implausibly hanging out, a black presence against our white sofa.

"You did what?" Jeff, acting that moment as a husband, not a therapist, shrieked the next morning as I recited the dream. "Don't let him in!"

"I need to. Death is a possibility. Why not face it?"

The legion of friends and family that came to visit over the months expressed only hope and optimism, but they surely knew, as did I, that my diagnosis warranted concern.

"What's it like to face death?" my friend Pat asked over lunch one day. I was relieved to talk about it.

"I'm no different from you, you know. Neither of us knows when or how we will die. Everyone faces death sooner or later. But, I will say, cancer has made that more real to me," I said.

As has happened to so many others, accepting death made life all that much more precious. On leisurely morning walks, I took up a favorite childhood pastime, looking up at the branches of the tree from the base of the trunk, imagining each branch with a story to tell. Putting up bird feeders, I started a list of all the species that visited. When Jeff spotted a Baltimore Oriole, I whooped in delight, ran into the house, found oranges and grape jelly and began to lure them close to our home. My piano playing, still possible before my injury, shifted to savoring the sounds of each of the keys.

"Press the key until you feel its base. Can you hear the difference? You're no longer striking the key. You're stroking it," Bob, my piano teacher advised.

"It's richer, more grounded. I feel more connected to the piano as an extension of my hands," I responded. Getting more into my playing, I explored the romance of Spanish music, the mystical beauty of Ravel and the intellectual, yet sensual appeal of Bach. The luxury of unscheduled days, thanks to my retirement from newspaper marketing, meant sleeping in with no alarm clock, spontaneous lunches with friends, and focus on my ever-expanding opportunity to work with women who faced major life transitions.

Buoyant that life had opened up in new ways and eager to share my experience, I started speaking to women's groups with a presentation called, "Dancing on the Glass Ceiling," declaring that now was the time to celebrate.

"At the end of every day now, I spend a few minutes in meditation, expressing gratitude. I always find much to be happy about. That's why I'm dancing these days, dancing for life and all that it holds out to each of us ready to see, to listen and to learn."

Yet, life with this new body has not been easy. The side effect of Taxol, one of the chemo drugs, was restless leg syndrome, due to the destruction of nerve endings. Within six months after treatment ended, my legs began to jerk uncontrollably, especially at night, which interfered with sleep.

"My breasts, my bladder, my bones and now my legs," I complained to an acupuncturist. The appearance of this problem felt like a new low, just as I was entertaining the joy of life post-cancer.

He listened sympathetically. Tears rolled down my cheeks as I curled up on his table. I couldn't bear the thought of him inserting needles right now in my beleaguered body.

"You can do this, Diane," he said, a comment I had heard throughout my life when my confidence lagged.

"Perhaps, but I'm tired—tired of more bad news, tired of being challenged, tired of gathering up my energy and resources to engage once more in the struggle to be healthy."

"Diane, you have very strong chi, very strong energy," he said. He was not one to offer gratuitous compliments, so I listened closely.

"The contrast between the person you were a year ago and who you are now is stunning. You're healthy, you just have a few limitations," he continued.

"I'm healthy," I told myself to test out the truth of this statement for me. I felt lighter just saying the words. "Yes, I'm healthy," I finally said aloud, now uncurling to open up to his treatment.

"You have choices to make about how best to use that energy. But for now, let's see what we can do about that leg pain."

I stretched out on the table, sighed, and wondered why life couldn't be easier. As he turned on the meditative music and dimmed the lights, I felt the stress begin to ease. And then, with the insertion of each needle, I repeated quietly, "I'm healthy. May this flow of energy be healing."

"One final thought, Diane," he said as he prepared the leave the room for me to rest. "Study Qigong. That will help you."

Hours later, I searched on my computer for

courses, workshops, articles—anything that would reconnect me to a practice I committed myself to more than ten years earlier but then dropped. "Qigong for Persons with Cancer" popped up almost immediately—a ten-day retreat in northern Montana with two Qigong masters from China. One was the chairman of the Cancer Tumor Research Committee charged with working with western doctors on integrating treatment strategies. Two weeks later, I was on a flight to Kalispell.

Purple-shrouded mountains encircle the valley. The sun has crept above the horizon signaling it's time to begin before the sun diminishes the early morning chi. Master Sun now waves us over to the lakeside. A short, solid man, dressed in a beige pajama-like garment, he demonstrates how we are to summon the chi using tonal sounds and movement. The healing energy will break through blockages in our bodies.

He stands with his back to us, facing the lake. Joining the thumbs of each hand with his middle fingers and placing his hands behind his back over his kidneys, thereby joining all of the energy meridians identified in Chinese medicine, he bellows the first tonal—"HAAA." The sound breaks the stillness of the morning. I stand straighter, brought to attention by the forcefulness of his voice.

Then the movement begins in coordination

with this tonal. He swings his upper body like a pendulum, ending with a "HAAA" that gradually becomes a laugh, "HA, HA, HA." He reverses the pendulum swing, now moving from right to left. His face, normally placid, becomes animated with energy. His eyes light with confidence and humor. His feet are firmly planted on the ground.

Ping, his interpreter, explains that the tonal we will make will be determined by the type of cancer we have. For breast tumors, the sound is "RUUU," ending in a boisterous "HUUU, HUUU, HUUU." Thumbs and middle fingers joined, hands placed beyond our backs, we swing in unison from left to right and then from right to left. Master Sun stands near each of us as we practice. Using his limited English skills, he says either "You right" or "You wrong" to signal whether our tonal is sufficiently robust. Sometimes he merely nods. He stands by me as I make my first "RUUU," nodding to communicate that I have correctly interpreted his instructions.

The power of the sound that comes out of my mouth startles me. It starts low in my belly, moves up through my chest and opens my throat wide. It's an exhalation with force—the taunt I've been searching for to beat back the doctors, drugs, needles and radiation machines that have subdued my body and spirit for nearly a year. "RUUU, RUUU...HUUU, HUUU!" So there. I'm still alive. This body is mine.

I become a warrior, warning off combatants

who dare to come close. I puff up, my feet pulling in energy from the earth and hurl my final "HUUU" with defiance to the mountains beyond the lake.

Master Sun says, "You right," as he walks by me. Then he demonstrates our final lesson, breaking into rapid and lyrical singsong Chinese, giggling and laughing, gesturing and moving his feet. Ping explains that he is telling a funny story. Through Ping, Master Sun now instructs us to return to Peaceful Lodge for breakfast and to tell a funny story to the acupuncturists and Chinese medicine doctors who have joined us this week to study Qigong.

"HUUU, HUUU," I chant as I sprint back to the Lodge, ready for the rest of my life.

After returning to Des Moines, I practiced this routine, complete with tonals, in the popular Rose Garden of the Des Moines Art Center. At seven every morning, just as the sun angled through the oak trees, casting shadows on the pink, lemon, cream and scarlet flowers, I planted my feet firmly on the grass, swung my body from right to left and then from left and right, and wailed my tonal. The fear and frustrations of the last year of surgery and treatment traveled with the sounds as they escaped my mouth.

"Are you all right?" the gardener who tended the roses came over to ask me after witnessing this routine for several weeks.

"More than all right. I'm feeling great. This practice is helping me heal," I explained.

"You just holler all you want," she laughed and went back to her trimming and pruning.

When Jesus reappeared in my life that morning, I knew he was not simply another stage in my religious development. This felt different. Could he have been there all along, a companion through all my life's experiences?

He had snuggled with me as a child, watched me explore the world, celebrated and grieved with me and patiently waited for me to accept his outreached hand. He forgave me when I didn't, rejoiced when I did. What mattered to me now was that he had a body, a whole body that had survived and triumphed over a tortured death. This was the Jesus I needed. This is why he came to me.

Suddenly I realized he *had* always been there, caring for me though doctors and dreams, through Qigong and acupuncture. I had come to believe in my *own* power to access energy, to heal my body through visualization, and to overcome obstacles. But finally, the increasing problems caused by spina bifida and the threat of breast cancer re-occurrence taught me that my powers were limited. I needed medical help and the complementary practices that support good health. Then, at the end of the day, or in this case at the beginning of the day, I also learned I needed and had been given grace—that undeserved love and healing power—from a generous, loving God. Jesus in all his physical glory invited me to dance in this wondrous reality.

As a response to his early morning visit, I enrolled in the Institute for Spiritual Guidance, a three-year program for individuals seeking to be spiritual directors. I enrolled, not only because I wanted to help others, but because I wanted to probe my deepening faith and more clearly understand it.

In my final paper for that course I declared, "The God Who Dances with my Spirit yearns for me, seeks ways to communicate with me, rejoices when I respond, and waits patiently when I am absent." Granted, the language was designed to impress my teachers, but the essence is true. My dancing, whether literal or metaphoric, has always been irregular and unconventional, but I have learned to return to the dance floor when my body or heart tells me it is time to grow, to reach beyond what is safe and known, to open up my heart to greater love, and to respond to the invitation of open arms. And there I dance.

WHERE SHOULD I START?

Seeing me stretched out on the couch, Angela teased me by saying, "You need a fainting sofa," as women gathered in my living room for Tending Your Inner Garden. I was preparing to introduce the next exercise at this fall retreat. But once again, back pain plagued me, making it difficult to sit.

"Yes, Marie Antoinette and I have so much in common. I should have been born in another era," I responded, picking up on her teasing. I fell back on the couch, put the back of my right hand on my forehead, exhaled a audible sigh and simulated the drama of "hysteria," a common diagnosis in previous centuries for women who exhibited "emotional excesses." Everyone laughed as they sipped coffee and ate the scones Jeff had baked for us that morning, soaking up the sun now streaming through the windows of the adjacent sun porch.

"Okay, let's get started," I said, taking the focus off me and back to the group. "Today we look at the importance of stories, the way they help give shape and meaning to events that otherwise feel random or inconsequential. By crafting stories, we reflect on what we have learned through our experience and share our accumulated wisdom with others." When I paused to catch my breath, one of the women broke in.

"But wait," Cheryl said. "We don't know your story. Why don't you start?"

"Yes," someone else said. "We know you have spina bifida, you mentioned that once before. But we don't know how that has affected your life. Is that why you lie down at our events periodically?"

Deb, my co-leader, and I sometimes share personal details about our lives with participants in the program, but only when it can be helpful as members grapple with addressing their particular concerns. Like other women, we've faced divorce, career change, illness and other crises that make our spirits wilt, but then open the door to new growth. We created Tending Your Inner Garden as a yearlong program in 2003 to guide women as they addressed such major transitions. But was this the time and place to talk about my journey with spina bifida?

"You're such a positive person, Diane," another woman said, offering encouragement. "You always look on the bright side of things. You're energetic. You don't let things get in your way. But it can't have been easy for you."

"I'll be glad to tell you more about me another time. For now, let's keep the focus on you." Feeling the old tension around talking about myself, I successfully redirected the conversation and put off the sharing of my own story to another time.

As the day progressed, I reflected on what I would say if they pressed me again. I could start at the beginning and share the details of my birth, including the fact that no one expected me to live. That would involve talking about the secrecy surrounding my condition, my parents' fear that I wouldn't go to school, and the challenge of managing a bladder that leaked. This story sounded sad, even unappealing, with all that leaking urine. However, my life, as I remember it, was far from that. I was a good student with an unstoppable curiosity about life, well liked, and I got through with surprisingly few accidents.

I could talk about throwing myself enthusiastically into my work—teaching high school English and Journalism (and, ironically, advising the high school newspaper, the "Telital"), running for political office, traveling the country as a political consultant, and serving as a marketing director and public relations spokesperson. This story featured excitement, adventure, and career success. Still, I was far from happy during those years. A need to prove myself as capable, worthy and independent drove my career focus, rather than a sense that my work was my actual life mission. My inner garden needed weeding then. The soil needed to be enriched with new nutrients. Perhaps there were even new seeds lying dormant, which, given time and space, would grow. Instead, I was out tending everyone else's garden—though not very sensitively or intentionally. That story would be easy to share.

Not so easy would be the story of my waking up after a nap to an image of myself encased in a cave wall, unable to move, victimized by some unknown source, constricted, resigned, sad, and unable to escape. The only way to break out was to grow so much from the inside that the walls dropped away. Could I tell that story in a way that communicated the terror of being trapped, the painful struggle to break free, and the irrational rage that still arises when someone surprises me by trying to fix me—perhaps correcting my make-up or straightening my necklace?

Imagining myself tending my inner garden helped me in that process, marking the emergence of a person who is, more often than not, able to express herself genuinely in the world. But would this story be too dark, too depressing to share? It might scare these women at the beginning of their mid-life journey even though I know that out of that experience came a new capacity for joy.

Breast cancer broke me wide open, showed me how much was bottled up inside and how the story about myself I'd been carrying for years was not really true. I thought I would die from spina bifida, and now I had cancer. I thought I could keep my body's problems a secret, but now I had a very public illness.

I thought I could get along without a spiritual life, but Spirit kept coming to me. I thought I could dictate the music for my life's dance, but the music kept changing.

Through my experience with breast cancer, I learned that the point of life is not to obsess about how I would die, but rather to decide how I would live. The encouragement of the women in my life (my sisters and my friends, as well as my ever-caring husband) had nurtured me to the point that I started to talk, to reflect more deeply, to journal, to open up and share what life was teaching me. Cancer gave me the final push I needed to make much-needed changes in my life.

Then I remembered my dream about death appearing at my door. Should I tell them about that? Would it be instructive or merely spooky? Perhaps we didn't want to talk about death on this bright sunny day when the mood was playful and light. On the other hand, inviting death into my life liberated me from anxiety. Yes, death would come. It comes to everyone. But death also enriches my life by reminding me of the preciousness of each moment and each day. Could this be shared without my sounding like a not-very-original new age guru?

I could tell them how these experiences freed my spirit and body to dance. The chronic bladder infections that troubled me for years stopped, as I began to realize, with the help of an art therapist, that the fear I carried inside was my father's fear, not mine. I could tell them about the dream I had in which my bladder came to my office door dressed as a thin, sickly woman in a short black and white servant outfit. The shock of that image, the realization that my poor bladder was tired of serving without appreciation or support, propelled me to revisit my incontinence. Would the group really want to hear about my bladder in this kind of detail? Probably not, but my struggle with my bladder is a clear example of how our emotions and unconscious life can affect our body's health, either positively or negatively.

I wondered if I should tell them the story about my big slip. Just weeks before, I had been entertaining a number of women in our home. I was rushing around, giving directions to the caterer when he asked, "As the hostess, do you have a special tea cup you'd like to use?"

Without a heartbeat I said, "You mean the one with the crack?"

He flinched and then realized I wasn't joking. Deep down, I chose the only defective cup for myself. Was I being a good hostess, keeping the good china for my guests, or was I somehow identifying with that cup.

He paused and then recovered. "Yes, that's often the way we think, isn't it?" he said with a forced smile as if he could read into my soul.

Embarrassed, I tried to concentrate on other matters regarding the luncheon. But the flash comment kept playing in my ear. Even after all the physical and spiritual work I had done over the years, still, when under stress, I equated myself to a cracked teacup. The girl with a break in her back. Perhaps it would always be so. Perhaps we all live with knee-jerk responses that never go away. The best we can hope for is that we will quickly see them for what they are—an old two-step we had learned so well we cannot forget it.

Would they relate to my story about Jesus coming back into my life? His reappearance helped me connect again with my beloved—this embodied divine man who reminded me to celebrate my body's sensuality, its capacity for pleasure, and its role in serving as God's presence in the world. Jesus reminds me daily of the Spirit's incarnation in nature, in the people in my life, in the globe that requires my tending to eliminate threats to its well-being. The Christian story of birth, death and resurrection is my story too. Or would this religious talk turn them off as it would have turned me off not too many years ago?

As I glanced around the room at their curious,

caring faces, I knew I would find a time and place to tell them about how my illness shaped who I have become today.

By recalling, probing and reflecting on my experience through the writing of this book, I am no longer that child who grew to be expert at keeping secrets, who rarely if ever talked about her disability, who planned her life as if that lump on her back where the surgery had taken place didn't exist, and who shied away from certain relationships and involvements for fear of her bladder's unpredictability. Deciding to revisit my past and then to share it has freed me from anxiety while increasing my gratitude for family and friends who have supported me in that journey. Beyond that, the process has fostered in me compassion for others and for myself.

These insights into my past have given me the grace to accept others who in their humanness made mistakes: parents who faced bewildering challenges and lack of support, doctors who through weariness or lack of knowledge offered little hope to me, and mostly myself for not loving this body enough, and for not tending my soul enough. I wish I had learned much earlier how to move through each day with acceptance, purpose, and joy. But I am thankful that that lesson has been taught over and over again.

When pain sets in, I now try to view it as the periodic visitor it is — one who occasionally limits my activities and requires me to adapt my plans, but does not have the power to limit my appreciation of this life I've been blessed with. Who would have guessed that a child born some sixty years ago and taken home to die would now be stretched out on this sofa as a mentor and guide to women gathered because they consider her wise?

As I pen these words, my mother's face comes to mind. "Diane, some day you will write about all this," she said. And I now do that, not only for myself and for my readers, but also for her. She struggled to live the life she imagined for herself and lived the life she was given. Her quiet courage and resilience inspired me to look lovingly at reality, to dance with it creatively, and to respond to the rhythm of divine music as it changes. And changes. And changes.

Acknowledgments

Many friends and family have danced along with me throughout my life and especially as I wrote this book.

Mary Nilsen, author, publisher and superb reader, worked as my developmental and content editor. She offered almost daily encouragement, feedback and inspiration, devoting more of her time than I could reasonably hope for. Without Mary, this book would not have been written.

My husband Jeff has nudged me to write over the years, believing I have something important to say. He never tired of my ruminations, speculations, and expressions of insecurity. During our meal conversations during the last two years, he challenged me with, "How *are* you coming with your book?" He challenged me to keep writing. I am grateful for his encouragement.

My parents, John and Helen Cox, traveled a lonely path in ensuring my survival from spina bifida, often not knowing what to do but moving ahead anyway. My sister Eileen Gamm compiled the family's genealogy that enriched the details of these pages. My sister Sue Avila (I still call her Susie) helped me recall the childhood experiences we shared.

Much appreciation goes to Pam Reese at the University of Iowa's Hardin Library for uncovering relevant history of spina bifida.

Many people have mentored me along the way. Kay Riley, spiritual director, helped me discover my vocation as a spiritual director. Jeannette Wright, art therapist, worked with me in understanding the emotional and psychological impact of my childhood. Mary Kunkel and Kathy Reardon (both spiritual directors) have been companions on my spiritual journey. Deb Engle and I have become so close as friends and co-creators of Tending Your Inner Garden that people frequently mix us up. I am fortunate to have worked alongside her for these last twelve years.

Many people generously offered to read a draft of my manuscript and offer suggestions, among them my early writing buddies Mary Gottschalk and Carol Bodensteiner; also Ruth Foster, Roy Nilsen, Norma Hirsch, Terry Schupbach-Gordon, Denise Essman, Madeleine Kelly, Kathy Reardon, Kay Riley, Adele VerSteeg, Deb Engle, Ann Mendleson, Megan Sorensen and Nancy Jones. Their careful reading caught many problems with chronology, missing information, and those pesky typos.

Thank you to all my loving, creative friends. They provided the background music that inspired me to write this book and gave me the help, energy, and encouragement to finish.

DIANE GLASS

Diane Glass's diverse career spans teaching, politics, corporate marketing, radio talk show hosting and, currently, spiritual direction and retreat facilitation. She served as Vice President of Marketing for the *Des Moines Register* from 1983 to 2000. In 2003, she co-founded Tending Your Inner Garden®, a program that has helped hundreds of women find new life purpose and meaning. She now works on the staff of PrairieFire, a program of spiritual formation at the Des Moines Pastoral Counseling Center.

Diane has published essays in *The Iowan,* in the *Des Moines Register* and in four books of women's writings themed to the seasons, books she co-edited as part of the Tending Your Inner Garden series of publications. In addition, Diane has written dozens of meditations for "The Bridge," an organization of writers who post weekly meditations on the Internet, and she published meditations in *Christ in Our Home,* a publication of Augsburg Fortress Press.

She served as president of the Spina Bifida Association of Iowa, chair of the Governor's Developmental Disabilities Council and led community efforts to improve housing, cultural opportunities and educational programming for underserved citizens.

She and her husband Jeff Means have a treasured family that includes three sisters, a son and daughter-in-law and two grandchildren, along with a wide circle of extended family members and friends.

This photo, taken in 1953, shows smiling Diane, flanked by her mother Helen and her older sister Eileen. On the left is her younger sister Susie and her father John.

Spina Bifida Treatment and Outcomes

Surgery

No one knows for sure what causes spina bifida but scientists believe that genetic and environmental factors act together to cause the condition. Treatment depends on the type of spina bifida. In causes of myelomeningocele, the most severe form in which part of the spinal cord and nerves come through the open part of the spine, the child is usually operated on within two to three days of birth. This prevents infections and helps save the spinal cord from more damage.

In some cases, surgery may be performed on the fetus. A study funded by the National Institutes of Health, started in 2003, compares prenatal surgery with postnatal surgery in children with myelomeningocele. The study, called MOMS (the Management of Myelomeningocele Study), suggests that the amount of nerve damage can be lessened if the open spine is closed early in the pregnancy. Premature birth is more common with prenatal surgery and can cause respiratory issues.

Prevention

The Spina Bifida Association asks women to take a vitamin with 400 mcg of folic acid each day during the years of their lives when they are possibly able to have children. Spina bifida can be detected before birth through a blood test during the 16th to 18th weeks of pregnancy, an ultrasound and maternal amniocentesis to look at protein levels.

Complications

Children and young adults with spina bifida can have mental and social problems. In addition they may require surgical interventions related to hydrocephalus and Chiari malformation. They also can have problems with walking and getting around or going to the bathroom, latex allergy, obesity, skin breakdown, gastrointestinal disorders, learning disabilities, depression, tendonitis and sexual issues.

Management

Children with spina bifida can lead full lives. Because of today's medicine, about 90 percent of babies born with spina bifida now live to be adults, about 80 percent have normal intelligence and about 75 percent play sports and do other fun activities.

The best way to manage spina bifida is with a team approach. Members of the team may include neurosurgeons, urologists, physical and occupational therapists, orthotists, psychologists and medical social workers.

For more information, contact the Spina Bifida Association of America at spinabifidaassociation.org.